To Julia

Thank You.

Standard Procedure

I appreciate your
on going Support and
encouragement.

Love You guys.

T. R.

Tony has done a brilliant job of laying out the basics, as well as taking you through the steps required to make sure you create the systems you need to catapult your business to the next level. This is the blueprint you need to grow your business in a smart, manageable way.

— *Chris Ducker, ChrisDucker.com*

Storytelling is one of the most powerful tools we can employ in order to help others learn - and retain - valuable lessons and info. Tony's storytelling and his ability to bring real-life situations into this book make it a great resource for anyone who is just starting out with creating systems and processes in their business.

— *Kate Erickson - EOFire.com*

Success does not choose, it is chosen instead. It is your opportunity to grab it with both hands and hold on to it - Tony's book gives you all you need to get your work life organised and effective systems put in place. This is THE way to success."

— *Izabela Russell, musicradiocreative.com, NMEU.com*

Tony Brown is the man! He has taken the time to carefully craft content that's applicable, and that works. I've been honored to watch this book go from idea to product, and I've witnessed Tony and his brand grow accordingly. His smarts and energy about systems and strategy is second-to-none! GET THIS BOOK! READ THIS BOOK! APPLY THE PRINCIPLES INSIDE! And watch the same effect happen in your world.

— *Chris Daniel, The Consultant in Jeans onechrisdaniel.com*

If your business relies 100% upon you turning up then you don't own a business, you own a job. There are many aspects that make up a successful business - including great marketing, branding, and customer service - but you need solid systems and processes to ensure that you can deliver great results every time. Fortunately for all of us Tony has created the ultimate guide on how to grow a reliable business, and allow us to spend more time running our business instead of working in it.

> — *Chris Marr - Award Winning Entrepreneur and Content Marketer - cmauk.co.uk*

Throughout the time I've known Tony, he has helped in a myriad of ways to make my business more efficient, more productive and more successful. His advice has changed the way I do business, from simple little process adjustments to fundamental changes to the way I work with clients. Tony is the master of systems and I've no doubt he can transform your business, no matter what stage you're at.

> — *Colin Gray - thePodcastHost.com*

In a volatile, uncertain, complex and ambiguous world everyone needs anchor points. In this book, Tony takes you way beyond anchor points! He sets out how you can take back control of your life, by systemising your work, reducing your workload, and increasing your productivity and profit. This book clearly and concisely sets out how to work and think smarter. I highly recommend this book.

> — *John Thurlbeck, John Thurlbeck Consulting - johnthurlbeck.co.uk*

Tony has proven that having Business Systems in place can allow you to have the freedom you desire whilst your business continues to run, uninterrupted.

— *Mr Matt Young, Making Social Media Work –*
mrmattyoung.com

For any business to be a success, it must be driven by a great leader whose foundation is built on systems that give them true leverage in order to scale and own a commercial and profitable organisation that works without them. In this book, Tony has laid out those fundamental steps for you to do this in your business now.

— *Leon Streete "The Lead Generation Coach",*
LeonStreete.com

I'll be honest. I was sceptical at first – after all, who knows my business better than I do? But Tony has helped me to identify the areas where I need to create standard procedures, which will only improve the service I deliver to my clients. I cannot thank Tony enough!

— *Neal M. Brown, @nmbrown, vitalitycopywriting.com*

If you feel overwhelmed by your Business and have never tried business systematisation, you are in the right place. Standard Procedure is accessible, actionable and packed with real life examples. Tony will hold your hand towards a business that works better and grows faster, without you exhausting yourself at it.

— *Coralie Sawruk, coraliesawruk.com*

If you haven't had holidays in 5 years, in fear that your business explodes in your absence - this book is for you. Tony lays out the basics of creating systems and procedures in your business in a way that is easy to understand and implement. What's more, it's not just for the new kids with techy startups - Tony's experience in systemising traditional business is what makes this approach to remote working unique - and relatable to any small business owner.

— Marta Krasnodebska, movabo.com

Tony has turned time consuming complex business systems into an easy to implement robust formula which will allow you to step away from your business and run it remotely. If you want to create systems to scale your business and have a freedom based lifestyle, look no further. This is exactly what you need.

— Petra Foster, Brand Wealth Strategist. PetraFoster.com

'It's not a lack of working hard holding new business owners back but overwhelm and unfocused work. That's where systems and procedures come in to save the day, transform your business and your life - and Tony will show you exactly how to do it.'

— Kathryn Bryant, Author & Podcast host,
BrilliantLivingHQ.com

Standard Procedure

How To Systemise Your Business
Reduce Your Workload
Increase Your Productivity
and Become Profitable

TONY L BROWN

TONY L BROWN MEDIA LTD

Attention Business Owners

This book is available for bulk purchases at special discounts. For information E-mail support@TonyLBrown.com

Thank you for supporting the hard work of this author.

To access all the additional resources mentioned in this book

visit: www.tonylbrown.com/spbookbonus.

CONTENTS

SECTION II : How To Create Your Standard Procedures - A Step-by-Step Process. 123

DEDICATION

To My Wife, Nicola

Thank you for telling me to stop talking about it, and just write it.

That was the most impactful piece of coaching advice I have ever received.

I love you and I plan to spoil you rotten.

To My Children, Shaniah, Jaziah, Zakiah and Naphiah

I love you all very much. But secretly love each one of you more than the other, in one way or another.

You bring me no end of joy and happiness.

I'm so blessed to be your dad.

Mom & Dad

I'm on a mission to repay you for the lifetime of investments you made in me.

I aim to give you the desires of your hearts.

Just give me a moment.

WHY YOU SHOULD READ THIS BOOK

I would like to introduce you to a friend of mine name Lloyd. If you can relate to Lloyd in any way, then there is something in this book for you.

Lloyd is 40 years old, He is married to Pamela. They have been married around 15 years. He is a father of three wonderful children. A 14-year-old daughter, 10-year-old son and a 6-year-old son. Lloyd and Pamela own their home and also have one rental property.

Lloyd is a small business owner and has been running his business for just over 5 years. The business is going pretty well and turns over between £50,000 and £70,000 each year.

Lloyd has worked hard to get the business to that point but recognises the negative impact his business is having on his personal life. Lloyd is busy running the business and wants more time to spend with his family. He feels like he is missing out on his children growing up.

He spends more time working in the business than he does with his family. Yet he started the business to free himself from the 9 - 5 routine so he could have more flexible time to spend with his family.

Lloyd and his family attend church each Sunday and enjoy helping out wherever they can.

Much of the business activity is dependent on Lloyd and if he were to go away for an extended period of time the business will eventually stop working. He has tried employing more people, but seems to spend more time managing them and showing them how the business should run. He feels trapped by his business.

He has also tried working a four-day week, but finds himself having a mountain of tasks to work through when he returns to work.

He often works late into the early hours of the morning, sometimes as late as 2-3 am. He then wakes up tired and sluggish. This has a negative impact on his mental and physical ability. Which then has its impact on his personal and work life.

Something has to change.

Lloyd fears that his business will ruin his marriage and that his children will grow to resent him because of the amount of time he spends running his business.

Lloyd knows that he needs to systemise the business but is unsure where to start. He has heard about the benefits other business owners are seeing from using online tools and automation but he is unsure on how to implement this into his business.

He knows that their is potential to grow the business, and he also wants to explore other new business ideas and opportunities, but he just can't take on any more work.

He wants someone to help him. He wants someone who can relate to what he feels. He wants somebody he can trust. Someone he can talk to not only about business matters but occasionally personal matters.

He wants his business to be able to run and grow without him and to be able to spend more time with his family and not worry about the business.

Lloyd has previously spent money on attending seminars and courses but has seen no real impact or change from doing this. He has never hired a business coach before but he knows and has heard that they are effective. He wants to be able to reassure his wife that any investment in coaching and consultancy will give them a good return on investment.

Lloyd is willing to invest in his personal development. But he is no fool and he's not going to part with his money easily and give it to any scamy Guru-like Internet marketer.

Lloyd enjoys reading and learning and has recently come across audiobooks on podcasts. He has started downloading these onto his mobile device. He has a few self-help audio books and biographies written by some well known entrepreneurs, business owners and investors. But he is still pretty new to the world of new media, content marketing, digital marketing and online entrepreneurship.

Both Lloyd and Pamela's parents have emigrated and now live abroad. Lloyd would love to have the freedom and flexibility from his business to take the family and spend regular and longer periods of time visiting their parents abroad.

If you can relate to Lloyd in any way, then you must read this book.

FOREWORD

I met Tony in summer 2015, he was a user of Process Street. We connected and I was a guest on his podcast. Since then, we've been working on the Business Systems Explore podcast together, which we launched in spring 2016.

As co-founder and CEO at Process Street, I have a lot of experience in dealing with poor processes in my own company and the pain that causes me, and now I also have the experience of working with thousands of companies from all around the world. I have heard so much from them about the pain caused due to poor processes, and then I have seen how much relief they get and time they recover by implementing effective systems.

I was the youngest CISCO engineer in Australia when I was only 16 years old. I have run multiple internet companies, including an e-commerce store, an affiliate marketing company that I built to over a million dollars in revenue in the first few years, and one failed start-up, and now, Process Street.

I started Process Street because when I was running my affiliate marketing company, I had a team of more than 20 people, three people in the US, an office in India, and a number of remote home-based workers in the Philippines. That setup became a nightmare to manage. I found myself, many mornings, up until six o'clock handling team enquiries.

That became a huge strain on me and was not the lifestyle I wanted. I needed a solution to fix it. That solution was the start of what Process Street has become.

The concept of building systems--the ability to implement a system via technology or a tool of some sort that can give you back your time--is at the core of what Process Street is.

Maintaining Standard Procedures has helped me most by giving me the ability to get so much more work done than would ever be physically possible without them. Even if I was to work 24 hours a day, seven days a week, I still would not be able to get as much done on my own.

Initially, I implemented Standard Procedures because I got to a point where I couldn't manage the volume of work on my plate, a point where I had no time for myself. It was a breaking point.

Now, Standard Procedures have helped me to achieve way beyond what would be physically possible on my own.

The importance of Standard Procedures varies, depending on where you are in your lifecycle of your business, your career, or your personal life. If you're just starting out as an entrepreneur and you're on your own, standard operating procedures are extremely important to put you in the mindset of scaling your business.

Standard Procedures help you figure out what work you're good at, and which gaps you need to plug. No business is perfect and by figuring that where your gaps are will help you understand who you need to hire and what types of systems you need to put in place in order to get the maximum impact.

To achieve growth in your business, you essentially need two things, systems and people.

If you're trying to scale your business with people, you're going to be much more effective by having systems in place because they allow the people that you hire to be more efficient.

As your business grows into multiple offices or multiple countries, you need to have processes in place to be able to manage that scale or those expansions will never work.

You can never truly scale a business that doesn't run on processes, and by implementing systems to scale, you're also implementing systems to sell. If you can scale your company you can step away from your company. Once your company gets to a point where it is ready to be sold, it's also ready to be stepped away from, and to run virtually on autopilot if you want it to.

This book will help you to develop an understanding of the importance of systems and developing a systems mindset. Not just for business, but also if you're trying to execute any kind of larger project that essentially involves more than yourself. Whether it's managing a school or the local football team.

Whether it's doing a charity project or organising an event. All of those things become more effective and efficient if there are systems in place.

Standard Procedures will ultimately make your business a more valuable asset as well as make you a more valuable individual because you're able to build and create things that are much larger than yourself.

This book will give you a step by step framework for how to build systems in your business, regardless of your starting point.

Vinay Patankar - Co-founder and CEO at Process Street

INTRODUCTION

I was encouraged by a number of writing coaches and other previously published authors to write a book that I want to read. Taking their advice, I never read book introductions.

I don't have patience for fluff. When I get a new book, I want to get straight to the meat.

Tell me the labor story later, just show me the baby.

If you do want to hear my backstory and get to know me more, then at the back of the book I have included the story that led up to this point. I think you'll enjoy it.

So, with that being said ... Let's move on.

SECTION 1

WHAT, WHY AND WHY NOT?

"The successful man will profit from his mistakes and try again in a different way."

— Dale Carnegie

Chapter 1

SCALE AND SAIL

Making a transition from being a full-time employee to a self-employed business owner was one of the scariest things I have done to date.

I could write a whole book about the internal battle I went through during that transition. Yet, once I'd made the transition and taken off the golden handcuffs, I was 100 percent focused on making my business work. Even so, this created a dilemma.

One of the main reasons I wanted to leave work was to be able to have more freedom and flexibility to spend quality time with my family. At the time of making my transition, my wife Nicola and I had been married for twelve years and we had four children.

I love my family and enjoy spending time with them. Being able to work for myself, on my own terms, would allow me to have more time to do that.

Yet, I found that the free and flexible time that I hoped for was becoming consumed by all the tasks I needed to do to make my business work. I found myself spending 12 to 15 hours a day working both in and on my business and this was becoming the norm.

Although I was working from home, I was absent more than ever, as I was in the office longer than I was when I was in my corporate job. I'm sure you can imagine the frustration. In fact, because you've picked up this book and are reading it, I know you know the frustration.

Out The Rat Race, Into Rat The Trap

I was working hard to get my business up and running and to get it to a level of sustainability and profitability. As time went on, I began to recognise the negative impact my business was having on my personal life and my family. I was spending more time working in my business than I was with my family. Yet, I started the business to have more flexible time to spend with my family.

Yes, I was able to enjoy breakfast, lunch and dinner every day with my family, which was a wonderful blessing. Yet, I wanted more. I felt trapped by my business and I began to feel anxious.

Would I make enough money to cover all our overheads?

Would I be able to provide for my family?

Have I made the right decision?

Have I done the right thing?

This anxiety caused me to work harder. I was often working into the early hours, trying to get things done. I would go to bed exhausted and unable to sleep as I could not stop thinking about work/my business.

What tasks do I need to do next?

What tasks are still incomplete?

What tasks are still on my To Do list?

Who do I need to contact?

After a night of little sleep, I would wake up tired and sluggish. This would have a negative impact on my mental and physical ability, which then had an impact on my personal and work life.

I began to fear that the business that I had created would, in time, ruin my marriage. I feared that my children would grow to resent me because I was spending so much time building and running the business.

Something Had To Change.

As a family, we love to travel and go on holiday together – even if it is just a simple road trip to the coast or a day out in the country. We love sharing those family experiences. What family doesn't? But I was struggling to find the time to make this happen.

I also knew that there was a lot of potential to grow my business and explore other areas of business. But with my current workload, I was unable to take on anything else.

I'd heard countless success stories from online entrepreneurs and internet marketers. All sharing the benefits that they enjoy from automating elements of their business and having Standard Operating Procedures (SOPs) in place which allowed other people to deliver elements of their business for them. People such as:

Chris Ducker

Virtual CEO, best selling author, podcaster, and speaker (and now a virtual mentor of mine), Chris was living like most entrepreneurs, working 14-hour days, six days a week, spending very little time with his family and working 'in' his business, instead of 'on' it way too much. After hitting the burn out phase, Chris made a radical change to his approach to business. He now deploys a huge team of virtual assistants to handle almost every moving part of his business empire. Chris has become the go-to guy in the area of "New Business and online entrepreneurship". He has built a massive global audience, whom he serves a regular stream of online content, which he has branded as "Value Bombs".

Chris only works an average of 6 hours a day, his workweek no longer includes Friday and he gets to spend lots of time with his wife and three children.

Pat Flynn

A thought leader in the areas of online entrepreneurship, digital marketing and lifestyle businesses. The creator of the Smart Passive Income Brand, which includes a successful blog, podcast and a Web TV show. He is a renowned speaker and author and has also created many spin-off products, including the Smart Podcast Player.

In his December 2015 income report, a monthly blog post in which he shares how much money he has made, Pat revealed that he had made a total Net profit of $71,757.47 that month. Not bad at all.

Michael Hyatt

The former Chairman and CEO of Thomas Nelson Publishers, the seventh largest trade book publishing company in the U.S. Now the author of eight books, including New York Times, Wall Street Journal and USA Today bestseller *Platform: Get Noticed in a Noisy World*. The founder of the online course "5 Days to Your Best Year Ever" and online membership community "Platform University", Michael also has a successful blog and podcast which you can find at www.michaelhyatt.com

John Lee Dumas

A former officer in the US Army who served for seven more years, including a 13-month tour of duty in Iraq. John is now the founder & host of Entrepreneur On Fire, a top-ranked business podcast where he interviews today's most inspiring Entrepreneurs, seven days a week.

John has created an online empire, including the EOFire Blog and Podcast, 2 membership communities with nearly 2500 members in total and a successful speaking career as an exclusive high ticket single person event.

John has become the flagship success story of what you can achieve online, earning a total Net profit of $2,950,579 in 2015, with an average monthly profit of $245,000.

Standard Operating Procedures

What do these guys have in common? They have all developed and implemented Standard Operating Procedures and built virtual teams to help build their businesses.

Those Standard Operating Procedures consist of checklists, detailed workflows, video walkthroughs, audio explanations, screencasts, infographics, quality assurance check sheets and anything else that would ensure that the tasks they delegate are executed to the same standard as if they would have delivered it themselves, if not better.

And all without them having to stand over their employee's shoulders and guide them through every stage of the process.

This demonstrated to me that by developing and implementing my own series of systems, I would be able to have processes in place which would allow me to step away from my business and even run it remotely.

The Turning Point

In early 2014, I successfully secured a contract to work with a group of students in a secondary school with the aim of supporting them to make better progress, achieve better results and ultimately recognise and reach their potential. The school required me to be on-hand throughout the school day for two days a week to offer group and one-to-one coaching to the students. Immediately, I knew that I could not commit that much time to one client.

I knew that my being out of the office for two full days a week would significantly impact the other areas of my business. During the negotiations with the client, I mentioned to them that it would not be me delivering the face-to-face work. I was pleasantly surprised by the response I received. She looked at me somewhat confused and said,

"Well, of course not. We wouldn't expect you to. You're the business owner. You've got other things you need to be working on."

I tried to maintain a shrewd businessman look on my face. Yet, internally, I was jumping around like a happy child who had been given access to the sweetie cupboard with no restraints. I left that meeting, headed back home and immediately started developing a series of standard procedures to enable my staff team to work effectively and achieve the same results that I would have worked to achieve. I created worksheets, exercise sheets, checklists, standard requirements and, put a handbook together for my staff to work through with those students.

That day, I made the transition from a freelance consultant to a business owner. That was the beginning of my freedom journey. Ever since that day, in early 2014, I've never delivered any face-to-face work in my youth engagement agency because I've had to. I've only delivered face-to-face work because I've chosen to.

Did It Work?

You're probably wondering, was the project successful? Well, I can tell you that our initial contract was for one term, approximately 10 weeks. We ended up delivering in that school for over a year and went on to deliver a series of different workshops to a range of different student groups, seeing great results each time.

My contribution to the project was to ensure that the staff knew which days they were working, what time they needed to be on site and meet with the clients near the end of each term to evaluate and review the work we were delivering. It was a wonderful feeling and I've never looked back since.

Knowing that for every hour I have a member of staff out in the field delivering to a client that they are generating an income for my business was fulfilling. I quickly realised that my job now is to get more staff delivering on more contracts. The more hours they work, the more money we earn. The key word here is scalability.

"Focus on being productive, instead of busy"

— Tim Ferris

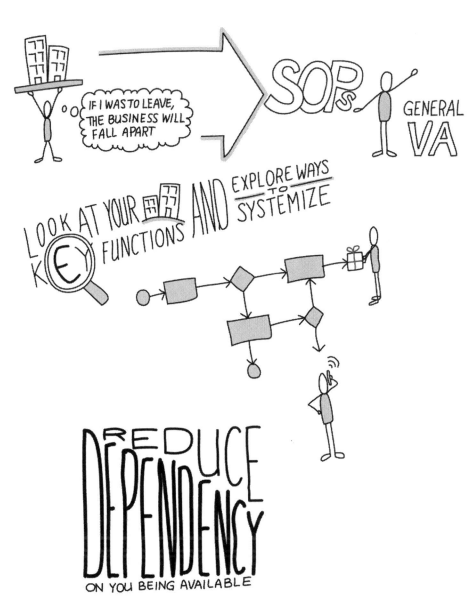

Chapter 2

I HAVEN'T HAD A HOLIDAY FOR 5 YEARS

One of the main reasons I've chosen to write this book is because I have spoken to a lot of small business entrepreneurs who are trapped by the business they have created.

While attending a business networking event, I got speaking to another business owner who had been in business for about 15 years. During our conversation, he said something that grabbed my attention.

He said, "I haven't had a holiday in over 5 years."

I responded, "Wow, 5 years, why not?"

He went on to tell me that he is too busy running his business to take a holiday. He told me that, "If I was to leave, the business will all fall apart as there is no one who could run it in my absence."

I thought to myself, "You poor guy."

I told him that I'd recently come back from touring Jamaica for eight weeks with my family, and I ran my business remotely while we were traveling. He gave me a look of disbelief. So I shared a bit of my story with him.

We didn't have much time left at the end of the event and I wanted to give him as much insight and information as I could because I felt somewhat sorry for him. I could see his frustration. I could see the upset and read the pain in his face. "I haven't had a holiday in over 5 years."

I dedicate this chapter to that gentleman.

These are the lessons learned from running my business remotely.

It's Not As Hard To Do As It May Seem

When you hear about people running their businesses remotely, most of the time they are online businesses. E-commerce stores or services that are delivered via the web. The business I had built was a traditional, hands-on business delivered by people.

I started Youth Work Toolbox in 2012. We are a youth engagement agency who provide staff to organisations who want to engage with young people more effectively. The business is based on a traditional employment agency model.

We have a small pool of youth workers and volunteers who are deployed to deliver a range of youth interventions and activities to our clients. When I started the business, I developed it so that it could be run remotely. My main aim was to work from home, yet I knew that we also wanted the flexibility to be able to travel as a family.

I developed and implemented a few key standard procedures which ensured that I didn't need to be around as much for the business to run. I employed an administrative assistant to help handle the inflow of general business enquiries and other admin tasks.

I would get a lot of phone calls, queries and emails, that I would handle and respond to. I knew that if we were going to be out the country, I would not be able to respond to them as quickly as I would like to. Or as quickly as the staff and clients were used to.

So I hired Leanne, my general virtual assistant.

The Virtual Assistant (VA)

When I first heard the term VA being used by other entrepreneurs, I thought they were referring to an app or a piece of software.

I've since learnt that a virtual assistant (VA), is a self-employed freelancer who can provide a range of professional, administrative, technical, or creative support to clients remotely, usually from a home office.

Job roles and tasks can vary among general administration, web development, graphic design, customer support, online marketing, social media management, bookkeeping and accountancy, research, content creation and promotion.

Because the VA is an independent contractor rather than an employee, you, as the client, are not responsible for any employee-related expenses, such as taxes, insurance or other benefits that are usually associated with having a direct employee.

Also, because the VA works remotely, you don't have the logistical problem of providing office space, equipment or supplies. So all you pay for is the work carried out by the VA, which can be an agreed hourly rate or a project by project agreement.

To communicate and manage my VA (which has now grown into a team of VAs) I make use of online tools such as Slack, Skype, Trello and even the mobile phone instant messaging app, WhatsApp.

My Initial VA Arrangement

I initially employed my current General VA, Leanne on a five hours a week basis to handle any incoming queries from both staff and clients. At the time of writing, Leanne is still working with me and she now has a 30 hour per week contract.

About eight weeks before we left the country, I spent some time training and preparing Leanne for the role. I provided her with some checklists, workflows, and other documents, and delegated a few tasks to get her used to the organisation, the business we do, the nature of the calls and emails we get.

As time got closer to us leaving, I increased her contract to 10 hours per week. Having Leanne in place relieved me of my concern of not being able to respond to staff and client enquiries.

The current contract we were delivering on was quite a high profile project, with a number of senior managers from a range of government and non-government organisations as stakeholders. I was worried that if I wasn't around and I didn't attend the meetings, it would impact on our brand and on our reputation around the table in the eyes of those stakeholders.

What's The Worst That Can Happen?

I almost allowed my fear of things going wrong in the project to prevent us from taking the trip. I discussed the matter with Nicola, and we came to the conclusion, "What's the worst that can happen?"

A partner meeting gets called and I don't attend or Leanne doesn't reply to an enquiry in the same way or timeframe as I would.

It's not the end of the world—and it's not unforgivable. As long as we deliver on our contractual obligations—provide a range of youth work interventions and activities to young people in a specific area and provide the partnership board with the necessary quarterly management reports—then there was nothing to fear.

The good news is, there was no drama. For the eight weeks we were away, nothing came up. There were no additional meetings, emergency phone calls, and no issues raised that Leanne couldn't handle.

While we were away, we were able to secure two new contracts from one of our existing clients, and a client for a new social media marketing agency that I'd only just launched. This worked out pretty well for us, as securing those three contracts gave us a nice financial cushion to come back home to.

Systemising Your Business Is Not As Hard As You Think It Might Be.

By developing and implementing a few standard procedures, you can significantly reduce the number of business functions that are dependent on you being available, which will reduce the amount of time you need to spend working in the business.

Take time to look at the key functions required to keep your business running. Once you have identified them, and documented them, explore ways you can systemise them.

Put procedures in place that will allow you to delegate work to somebody else, or even automate the process. In return, this will give you the time you need to do other things.

To access the worksheet related to this chapter visit: www. tonylbrown.com/spbookbonus.

"If you don't drive your business, you will be driven out of business."

— B. C. Forbes

Your Business is a Series of Systems

Chapter 3

LESSONS FOR LOCATION FREEDOM

A Business Is A Series Of Systems.

Your business systems are the cogs in the machine that make your business work.

If you think about a car, the engine is a series of systems all working together to make the car work. Consider the human body. It's a very complex machine, but it's a series of systems all working together to allow the body to function. Your business is exactly the same, it's a series of systems.

In preparing to go away, I had to undertake the process of documenting all the standard procedures for a newly appointed admin assistant. Now, a lot of the procedures already existed, but they were not documented, they were in my head. I would carry them out when required and never took the time to document them.

Gaps In The System

There were also business functions that my wife, Nicola, who is also my finance director, would do throughout the month, specifically related to payroll. We had a payroll procedure and other such things in place, but we never had them thoroughly documented anywhere. She would just carry them out. If we had to delegate those tasks to somebody else we would still have to be very much around to guide them through the process.

We had to go through a process of documenting these standard procedures to be able to delegate to Leanne. A few of them we knew off the top of our heads, so that process was pretty straightforward. Others, we had to develop from scratch as they were based on "What If's". We had to consider the response and desired course of action we would want Leanne to take to a number of different potential situation that may arise. We had to go through those scenarios and create a process of "If this, then that."

If a member of the staff calls and is unable to attend a session, then what do we want to happen? If a client calls and is requesting specific information, then what should happen? Now what would previously happen, is that I would consider the options on the fly, make a decision and respond. But for this to work, we had to map out what should happen in each of these scenarios.

We'll cover the actual process of developing systems in section 2. I will take you through the entire process from the initial brainstorming all the way through to implementation.

I can't emphasise enough the importance of having documented systems and processes that govern your business activity. Once you can document every process for every function in your business and document it in a way that someone who has never done the job before can follow that procedure and complete the task to the required standard, then you've hit the nail on the head and you're ready to go.

Train Your Clients

You can create a system to train your clients to not expect to see you for a while. Now I know "Training your clients" is not language some people are comfortable using.

When I started Youth Work Toolbox, my intention was to be a virtual company.

We work from home, and unless it's absolutely necessary, I very rarely leave the house.

It's not because I'm a recluse. It's because we're very family-orientated. I've got four children. I'm married and I want to be here at home with the family. If I do need to have a face-to-face meeting, then very often we'll meet at a local art gallery or a café somewhere or I'll go to the office of the client.

We hold a lot of meetings on Skype. Whenever possible, I would try to arrange a meeting via phone call, conference call or Skype. The intention here is to get the client used to communicating with me like that, communicating with me remotely, so that when you are working remotely, it's not a big transition.

They become accustomed to not seeing you or to your contacting them via email or sending them a Skype message. They are not suddenly going to think, "Well, where's Tony gone? How come I haven't seen him for 3, 4 weeks? What's going on? Why has he suddenly started only sending me emails?"

You can train your clients to not expect to see you for a while.

Now, a few weeks before we were scheduled to fly out, I sent emails out to all my clients and introduced them to Leanne. I shared with them our new communications protocol that we developed and that this is now the procedure. Leanne would now be the first point of contact for business enquiries.

Rather than them emailing me, I made them aware that now they must contact Leanne. If Leanne can't handle it, she would then escalate it up to me. And that worked fine. It was great. There were no issues. None of the clients asked any questions. It was business as usual.

Great Escalation Saves A Nation

In the project management world there is a management principle referred to as "Manage by Exception". If you're not familiar with the PRINCE2 project management method then you will most likely not have heard this term before. Yet, once I've explained the method, it is likely that you will recognise that you have used this approach many times before.

The Manage by Exception principle provides each management level with a system to manage and control the lower management level so that they don't need to be bothered by small issues that arise. When used thoroughly, the project management board will include what are called tolerances, which are a set percentage increase or decrease related to project cost, timeframe or other variables.

For example, the cost of the project is projected to increase by 10% or the timeframe is likely to increase by 20 percent. Those percentages are called Tolerance. If you have a project of developing a new website, you delegate the role of Project Manager to your general Virtual Assistant. The other team members and freelancers contributing to the project will report to them.

If everything is going fine, you won't hear from the Project Manager except for the regular updates you've agreed upon during each stage and at the end of the stage. Unless there is an exception above the agreed tolerance level. If the problem is small and it remains within the tolerances e.g., the costs increase by only 2 percent, then the Project Manager can handle it and doesn't have to alert you and take up your time.

This is great as it empowers the Project Manager to just get on with the task, and take the necessary action that they believe is appropriate. Rather than having to keep checking with you.

Train Your Staff

Similar to the last point, you can also train your staff to not expect to see you on a regular basis. Within most traditional businesses, team members and managers are usually based in the same building and sometimes in the same room or office. Also, most recruitment and training of staff is done in person.

Yet, I knew that this would not suit the business model I was developing. I did not want to be tied to a fixed location or have to travel to an office every day. Nor did I want to spend my time interviewing people. In my past corporate job, I have spent 3 full days—and I mean FULL DAYS: 9:00 am-9:00 pm—conducting staff interviews, and being out of the office for that amount of time, causing a backlog of work for me to return to.

Virtual Recruitment

What I have implemented has allowed our entire staff recruitment process to take place online, and not just for my virtual staff member, but also for our youth work staff.

All our staff interviews are conducted via Skype. We'll have a video call and conduct the interview process as though the person was in the same room as us. Given that it's the year 2016 at the time of writing this, this should not be such a big deal, but I'm still surprised at how many businesses are still not making the best use of the online tools available.

Make Use Of The Tools Available

I've mentioned Skype a few times already as it is one of the tools that has played a big part in making our business model work.

I've been using Skype in our business for a long time. It has become part of our communications protocol. Not only is being able to make Skype calls to clients, both existing and potential, very cost efficient, but also having a Skype landline number with a local area code, that we can divert to another number, anywhere in the world, that is a big bonus.

Calls can be diverted to a mobile phone while you're in another country or they can be diverted to a team member elsewhere. And the cost of this is very reasonable.

The benefit of conducting this process online is that we can get interviews done much quicker and cheaper than if we conducted them in person. The candidate doesn't have to worry about traveling and parking, and the risk of getting caught in traffic or being late.

For us, we don't need to incur the cost of hiring a venue or a room, and going through the process of setting the room up, making sure everything looks proper and presentable, having refreshments available and having to manage the arrival of candidates. In previous recruitment drives I have managed, these things can become a logistical nightmare.

With an online video interview, each candidate gets a timeslot. They will be contacted a few minutes before that time to check to see if they're ready and then we call them. I know for some staff, being interviewed via a video link can feel strange, but it's worked well and I've had no complaint about the process to date. It did feel risky at first, but you have to go with what you believe to be right for your business. That's the process we've adopted and embedded, and that's what we're running with.

Staff Enquiries

Previously, I would receive a lot of general low-level enquiries that would end up consuming my time, or just taking my focus away from other tasks I should be handling. I would get calls, text messages, emails about low-level minor issues such as I can't find the timesheet or I can't access Google Drive or my timesheet is not adding up correctly or where is the session taking place this evening?

As with my clients, I sent a staff newsletter around a few weeks before we left the country. In it I included a section introducing Leanne to the team, and explaining the new communications protocol and procedure. This made the staff aware that Leanne would now be the main point of contact for general enquiries and if she can't deal with your enquiries then she would escalate it up to me.

I did make it clear to the staff that if there were any health and safety concerns or anything related to safeguarding children and young people, then that should come directly to me. But as for everything else, shoot over to Leanne in the first instance.

It took a while for some members of the staff to catch on as they had become so used to contacting me. When I did get those calls, the first thing I said to them is "Have you called Leanne?"

Think Ahead

During the planning stages of Youth Work Toolbox, location independence was something that was at the forefront of my mind. When making decisions about buying office equipment and other resources, I had to keep in mind the fact that I wanted to be able to move around easily, without having to drag a ton of equipment with me.

I was always thinking about it. What if we want to move? What about when we're on the road? What about when we fly?

I don't even like carrying a load of suitcases with us on holiday, but when you've got four children, traveling light becomes a real challenge. I was sure that I didn't want to be carrying around big, bulky pieces of equipment.

For our main office computer, I bought a Mac mini, which is about 20cm by 20cm square and approximately 3.5cm in height. I know I could carry this with me anywhere. It was powerful enough to handle all of my multimedia needs, and could be hooked up to monitors and TVs with a HDMI cable, whether in a hotel room or my parents' TV room. The mini keyboard and trackpad meant I had full functionality on-the-go.

I bought a small, hardbacked suitcase on wheels and simply slipped the Mac mini in there with my wireless keyboard, trackpad, a USB camera, and other bits and pieces. I was able to carry the case on the flight with me.

We both have iPads which we use mainly for consuming media, and they were great for catching up on the occasional email and social media updates.

We more or less had everything we needed to run the business in one small carry on suitcase.

Other Things To Consider

You need to be aware that when you go to another location, home or abroad, you may, and probably will, encounter internet speed and connection problems. I have even encountered unforgivable internet services at major hotel chains here in the UK.

Three's A Crowd

Once I got my workstation set up at my parents' house in Jamaica, I did a preliminary test run. There were some initial connection problems, but once I got online, it all seemed to work fine.

Yet, as time went on I found that the Internet kept on disconnecting. What I realised was if two or more other devices were trying to log on to that wireless box at the same time it would overwhelm the router and it would log off one of the devices. It was first come, first served. Whoever was logged on first, they were getting the connection. I had to make an agreement with everyone in the house that while I was working, everyone would have to turn off the wireless on their devices.

Once I overcame the connection hurdle, the next mountain to climb was the slow internet speed. If you're like me, I'm sure you've become accustomed to having access to your superfast broadband connection. I totally take mine for granted.

Super Slow Internet

My entire family, and there are 6 of us, can all be surfing, streaming and downloading, and we never notice any significant impact on the speed of the Internet. In Jamaica though, it was a different matter. For general emails and browsing the speed wasn't that noticeable. It was obvious that it was slower than what I'm used to back home, but it wasn't really a big issue.

Yet, on one occasion I tried to upload a short video blog to my YouTube channel and it was at that moment I realised we had a problem. The video was probably only about five or six minutes long of standard quality. We're not talking high definition here. I make no exaggeration, it took almost 12 hours to upload that short video.

I started the upload in the evening and I must have sat there for about two hours as it was processing and uploading. It got to the point where I decided to go to bed and leave it to upload.

When I woke up the next morning and checked and it was still processing, I could not believe it! Back home, I could upload multiple videos in a few minutes. In fact, I can have multiple videos all uploading at the same time, and it'll all be done in less than 10 minutes.

You may not be planning to tour the Caribbean for eight weeks, but I want to encourage you to take the time to develop and implement standard procedures which will allow you to leave your business for a significant amount of time without it grinding to a halt.

Put standard procedures in place so that your business is not dependent on you turning up every day to be on hand to make things happen. It's not as hard as you think it might be.

Questions:

As long as you think ahead and plan ahead it's very possible that your business can run without you.

What actions can you take to begin to get your customers or clients used to not seeing you as regularly as they currently do?

What actions can you take to begin to get your employees used to not seeing you as regularly as they currently do?

What tools and apps (both free and paid) could you make use of right now to help you be more mobile friendly and location independent?

What business functions could you quickly and easily delegate or automate to remove you from the workflow?

To access the worksheet related to this chapter visit: www. tonylbrown.com/spbookbonus.

"The common question that gets asked in business is, why?

That's a good question, but an equally valid question is, why not'"

— Jeff Bezos

WHY YOU SHOULD SYSTEMISE YOUR BUSINESS
IN SHORT, TO MAKE YOUR BUSINESS WORK!

THE E MYTH
M.E. Gerber

o SYSTEMS
o FRANCHISE
o SELL (ABLE)

START WITH WHY
Simon Sinek

 CLEAR GOAL

A BUSINESS THAT WORKS
WITHOUT THE BUSINESS
OWNER PRESENT.

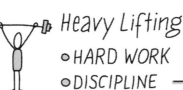

Heavy Lifting
o HARD WORK
o DISCIPLINE

#1

BUILD A BUSINESS THAT WORKS
FOR YOU, NOT A BUSINESS
YOU WORK FOR.

Chapter 4

WHY YOU SHOULD SYSTEMISE YOUR BUSINESS.

I f you were to ask me why I systemised my business, my first response would be that I read a few books that changed my entire perspective on business. Those books introduced me to the concept of systemising and franchising a business. Over the last 4 years, I've taken the principles I learned in those books and applied them successfully to my business. Now I'm going to show you how you can do the same.

The E-Myth

One of those books is *The E-Myth* by Michael E Gerber. This book has been on the business best seller list for probably almost 20 years, if not more, and has sold millions of copies worldwide. The core theme of *The E-Myth* is creating a business that is systems dependent rather than people dependent. A business that is governed by a series of systems that can be executed by other people. Michael puts forth a strong case as to why you should systemise your business and I highly recommend you read that book, if you haven't already done so.

It will give you a good foundation in which you can start to implement some of the practical steps you'll find in this book. Michael also explores the concept of creating a franchise. Developing your business as though there will be many other businesses just like yours running all around the world. He also introduces the idea of building your business as though you're going to sell it. Many of these concepts are overlooked by small business owners when they are developing their business. Often they want to get in there, get it off the ground, and start making money.

The subtitle of *The E-Myth* is "Why Most Small Businesses Don't Work and What to Do About It". The answer to the question, "Why should you systemise your business?" is found right there in that subtitle. Most small businesses don't work and there's something you need to do about it. That something is systemisation.

As a business owner, your time is better spent doing the high-level tasks that only you can do. Tasks such as business growth, strategic planning, systems development and improvement, building and maintaining employee and client relationships, content creation, new product innovation and so on. What you should not be doing is focusing on the technical, on the ground, face-to-face delivery of your products and services. But I'll get more into that a little later on.

You Need To Know Why You Want To Systemise Your Business.

Before you take any action towards systemising your business, the first thing I encourage you to do is to have a very clear end goal. There is a saying that has become popular recently amongst marketers and entrepreneurs, and that saying is: "Start with why". There is also a book by Simon Sinek with the same title.

What starting with *why* means is that your starting point for anything, but specifically in business, should be a very clear reason as to why you're doing what you're doing. Once you're clear on *why*, you'll then know how. Your *why* will determine the best course of action to take to obtain the *why*.

I shared my *why* in chapter one. I wanted to have more free and flexible time to spend with my family. I wanted time to do the things I wanted to do. And there's nothing wrong with that because that was my *why*. Take some time to brainstorm and to reflect on what you want as your end goal.

Find Out What Your *Why* Is.

Now your *why* will be very different than mine. You must be honest with yourself, because ultimately it's your *why* that's going to drive you to put in the time, effort and energy required to create the business procedures that you need to put in place to free you from your business.

After coaching and consulting small business entrepreneurs for a few years now, I've found that there is a noticeable pattern when it comes to identifying end goals. The one that comes to the top more often than any other is the end goal to have a business that runs effectively without the entrepreneur needing to be present.

To have a business that runs successfully regardless of whether the business owner is there or not.

Another popular **why** is for that business owner to be able to leave their business for up to six months and come back to find that the business has grown. The main theme here can be boiled down to this: The entrepreneur wants to own a business and not have to work for anybody else. They want to reap the benefits of being an entrepreneur, and ultimately have the freedom and flexibility to do other things. To do the things they want to do, whatever those things may be.

Having A Very Clear Reason Why

What's your end goal? What's your **why**? I tell my coaching clients that answers such as "I want to be rich" or "I want to be successful" is not enough.

You need to be very clear on why you have the goals you have. Having a very clear **why** will help to keep you motivated when you hit a barrier or a blockage, and when things get tough. And trust me, they will get tough. The work of systemising your business is not a walk in the park. If it was, everybody would do it, but everybody doesn't do it.

The entrepreneurs that understand these principles and are willing to put the hard work in, and have the discipline to develop and implement the procedures required, are the ones who see massive success and reap the benefits of having a business that works for them.

The mistake that a lot of entrepreneurs make is that they have an idea for a business or an opportunity presents itself, and they start running with it. One task leads to another task, and one project leads to another project. As the idea starts to develop and grow, so does their workload. The entrepreneur then finds themselves overwhelmed working on a number of projects and executing a number of tasks related to that project. Although those ideas they have may be viable, and might even be successful, they may not necessarily be in line with the entrepreneur's end goal.

The Opportunity That Didn't Match My *Why*.

Just as I was about to make the transition from employee to business owner, an opportunity was presented to me by a friend and business colleague. We knew each other very well, and had a history of working together successfully on previous projects. He had been self-employed for almost five years and had built a very strong personal brand and a successful consultancy business for himself. He's doing pretty well. He had built a strong business network around him and was very well positioned to do great things.

When he approached me to come on board and support the work he was doing, I jumped straight in with two feet, because I saw it as a great opportunity and feared I would miss the boat. I got straight involved and began contributing to a number of projects and leading on a few particular elements. I found myself putting in substantial hours each week to ensure that deadlines were met. As the months went on and the project began to develop, I began to recognise that what was being built was not in line with my end goal. His **why** and my **why** did not align.

Realising My Mistake

The vision my colleague had for his business was huge, and I admire his achievements. However, as my role in that business began to get clearer, I knew it was not something that I would be totally happy doing in the long run. It was as though we were recreating the job role that I was trying to escape from in my corporate employment. The only difference was that I would be working for my friend's company.

I had to make a very tough but honest decision and step away from that project and focus my time and attention on working towards my own end goal. I knew that the only way I would be able to achieve that end goal was by building my own business in a way that I saw fit for it to be built. To build a business that would serve me, rather than me serving the business. A business that worked for me, instead of me working for the business. One that could scale and grow without me having to be there every day, turning the wheels.

My business may not be as big and well-established as other businesses, but as long as it allows me to achieve my end goal I'm happy with that.

The first step of systemisation is to be very clear on what you want to build and why you want to build it. Know your end goal; be honest with yourself. Only know what your end goal is. This is your opportunity to be selfish, but for a good reason. Before you do anything else, take some time and identify and define your end goal.

To access the worksheet related to this chapter visit: www. tonylbrown.com/spbookbonus.

Questions:

Why is the goal you're working towards important to you?

What do you want as a result of achieving this goal?

Who will benefit when you achieve this goal?

What will things look like when you achieve your goal?

What do you want your life to look like in 30 years?

Health:

Family:

Home:

Time:

Work / Business:

Financial:

Spiritual:

Other areas relevant to you:

What is your definition of success?

If you had to volunteer for 6 months, where/who would you choose to serve and why?

If you had access to unlimited funds, what charity would you start and why?

Now that you've answered all the questions, go back to the top and read through your answers again. Reflect on your responses.

In one paragraph, summarise your main motivation/drivers— What is your **why**?

To access the worksheet related to this chapter visit: www. tonylbrown.com/spbookbonus.

"Working hard and working smart sometimes can be two different things."

— Byron Dorgan

SYSTEMISING DOES <u>NOT</u> MEAN ABDICATING

IT MEANS 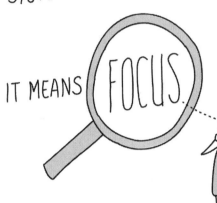 FOCUS ON YOUR ACTUAL ROLE:

BUILDING & GROWING YOUR BUSINESS

DO THE THINGS ONLY YOU CAN DO

REINVEST YOUR TIME SAVED.

 automate to improve, not just automate

☐ CUSTOMER ENQUIRY RESPONSES
☐ RECRUITMENT ENQUIRIES
☐ INBOUND CLIENT SCREENING

Chapter 5

SYSTEMISING DOES NOT MEAN ABDICATING

I was speaking to a prospective client about the work I do to help business owners to systemise their business. He was a business owner himself who ran a successful car leasing business. He'd been running his business for 12 years and shared very openly and honestly about his frustration at being overwhelmed by having to run the business on a day-to-day basis.

I shared with him my processes for systemising a business in a way that would enable him to not have to be around, yet still allow the business to continue to run. He pushed back and challenged me, saying:

"Am I not just neglecting my responsibility as the business owner and abdicating from my position?"

Although I was taken aback slightly by his response, I understand where he was coming from. The picture that was painted in his mind was that by systemising the business, you as the business owner and entrepreneur are just delegating everything to somebody else and having no input in the day-to-day running of the business.

Off you go, socialising down the pub or travelling around the world, leaving the work for your employees to do and if things go wrong, it's their fault.

You've Still Got Work To Do

Let me be clear. When I'm talking about systemising your business, I'm in no way, shape, or form encouraging you to abdicate from your responsibilities. In fact, the opposite is true, and your standard procedures will allow you to focus more on your actual role and responsibilities as the CEO of your company. You are still very much responsible for the success, development and growth of your business. You still have work to do. You are still very much accountable.

This is a big misconception a lot of people have. We hear about all these tools and apps which enable you to automate your business. Many of them I use and I recommend that my clients make use of them also. However, I don't subscribe to the notion of automating your business to a point where you don't need to have to do anything, that you just set it and forget it.

I know for some business functions this is fine. I also know that for some online entrepreneurs, this is the goal. To build a system that is totally automated and all you do is turn the machine on and wait for the emails from PayPal to start ringing. As I said,

I'm not against this. For some business models, this type of system works very well.

I do believe that, regardless of how much automation you use and how much systemisation you put in place, you still have overall responsibility for the success and growth of your business.

Doing The Work Only You Can Do

The only difference is where is your time is being spent. Your time should be spent building and growing the business, looking for ways to improve and refine your standard procedures, looking at ways of helping your employees and team members to develop and grow, looking at ways to refine your brand and increase brand equity, looking for opportunities to increase revenue, identifying ways that offer more value to your target market, and ways that you can better serve your target market.

Your time should be spent doing the things only you can do. Focusing on your business type and your business model will determine where your time is spent. Although you may find that through developing and implementing standard procedures you have much more free and flexible time on your hands, this does not mean that you should squander that time.

It does not mean that you no longer have responsibilities and accountabilities related to your business. Just be very wise where you choose to reinvest the new time you now have. Don't make the mistake of abdicating from your responsibilities.

Only Use Automation To Improve The Process.

With all the technology today, many people make the mistake of thinking that automation will automatically make something better. Yes, in many cases automation can improve a process if it is appropriate. However, you need to be very aware that automation can make a process worse.

In a blog article called "Sales Productivity Secret: Automation Isn't Enough", Brandon Redlinger—Growth leader at PersistIQ shares this dilemma ...

"How do you balance automation with personalisation?" He goes on to say:

"Automating too much of the process can actually set you back in terms of productivity. If the ultimate goal is to close deals and increase revenue, some interactions require a level of personal attention that automation can't (and very often shouldn't) provide."

And he's right! We are human beings—and people like to deal with other people. Virtual CEO and author of *Virtual Freedom*—Chris Ducker calls it p2p (person 2 person). I strongly support automation, but I'm also a people person. So I guess you could say I'm a bit of a cyborg.

The Twitter DM Of DOOM

One example of a poor use of automation is the Direct Message in twitter. I hate this. You follow someone and within about 5 seconds you get a Direct Message from them saying ...

"Hey thanks for following me. why not check out my XYZ ..."

What?? Everyone knows it's automated. The idea of a DM is that it is from you to me or me to you. It's meant to be a personal touchpoint. The worst thing is that oftentimes the main culprits are people claiming to be digital/social media marketing experts. Get lost - Unfollow!! - (I know - It's harsh)

A few things that I found work well automated are:

Customer Enquiry Responses

A simple acknowledgment that your enquiry has been received and is being looked at.

This auto response could include a link to a document that provides answers to your most frequently asked questions, a playlist of tutorial videos or audio podcasts and links to other useful articles.

Recruitment Enquiries

A candidate submits a completed application form for a post you are recruiting to. They then receive an auto response signposting them to a webpage with an online test they must complete which forms part of your shortlisting process.

This could include a video or audio welcome and introduction, followed by the instructions of what they need to do next. It may take a little time to put it together at the front end, but it will save you a ton of time later on down the line.

Inbound Client Screening

Someone in your target market lands on your website. They have a look around, read your latest blog post, and begin listening to your most recent podcast episode. While listening, they decide that you would be a good candidate to provide the solution to their problem.

They click on your "work with me" link in your navigation menu and view your products and services.

Now convinced that you are the right fit, they want to make contact with you.

On your "work with me" page, you have a big button that says "I'm interested" or "Let's work" or something along those lines. Your prospect clicks the button and is taken to an online client screening questionnaire that has been developed in Typeform or Google Forms. A list of questions that they must answer which will allow you to assess if the prospect meets your ideal client criteria.

Once they have completed the questionnaire and it is submitted you or your appointed administrative assistant, you will receive an email containing all the information you need to make a decision as to whether you will proceed any further with this prospect.

Automation should only be used to better something. Just don't overuse it. At the time of writing this, I recently heard about one guy who was on a mission to automate everything that takes him more than 90 seconds of his time—that's a bit much if you ask me!

Questions:

If you had a free 10-hour block of time each week, how and where would you reinvest that time?

What are the top 3 major functions in your business that only you can do.

What business functions could you automate now for maximum impact?

What business functions if automated would have a negative impact on your business?

To access the worksheet related to this chapter visit: www. tonylbrown.com/spbookbonus.

"There are no secrets to success.

It is the result of preparation, hard work,

and learning from failure."

— Colin Powell

REASONS YOU SHOULD HAVE STANDARD PROC

EMPLOYEE

FREELANCER*

OWNER

*free, but with a growth ceiling

#1 Consistency

#2 Efficiency

#3 Quality

#5 Clear Expectations

#4 Monitor & Evaluate

#6 Continuity

#7 Opportunity

Chapter 6

VALID REASONS YOU SHOULD
HAVE STANDARD PROCEDURE

Any entrepreneur who claims to have a business, but that business is not built on a series of standard procedures, which allow someone else to pick up and continue the work, does not really have a business.

There is a big difference between being a self-employed window cleaner and running a window cleaning business.The self-employed window cleaner goes out for 8 hours each day, cleaning windows to generate an income. The entrepreneur who runs a window cleaning business generates their income by having standard procedures in place that allows them to deploy any number of window cleaners to clean windows on their behalf.

Entrepreneur Or Freelancer

If, as an entrepreneur, you are the only person who can deliver those products and services or solve that problem, you don't have a business. You're a self-employed freelancer. For some readers, this may be a hard pill to swallow, but it is the truth.

You're still trading your time for money. Meaning that when you stop working, then income stops generating. That's a huge problem because you're very limited on the number of clients you can serve, and the amount of time you can spend on servicing those clients which would also limit the amount of income you can generate, so you only have two options:

Option One: Work harder, faster, longer

Option Two: Charge more for the services you deliver.

For each one of those options, there is a ceiling. There are only so many hours in the day. If you pick the other option, there is a ceiling price to what your clients will pay for the service you deliver.

A business is a series of systems working together to create a specific product or service to solve a certain problem. Here are some valid reasons why you should use standard procedures.

1. Standard procedures will ensure that there is consistency in the products and services you provide.

Having standard procedures ensures that you deliver the same service at the same high standard to every customer, ensuring that your brand maintains its integrity at every level.

The Restaurant

Try to imagine sitting in a restaurant with your significant other. There is a couple seated at a table next to you. You both arrived at the same time. But you notice that the waiter is already taking orders for drinks from the other couple, but you haven't been asked or seen to yet. The other couple have been giving some complimentary starters which you weren't offered. As the night goes on, you begin to realise that the couple across from you are getting a much better service than you seem to be getting. At this stage, you don't say anything as you don't want to cause a fuss.

As the night draws to an end, you realise that the other couple have received a significantly higher level of service than you have, so, you ask the waiter if you can speak to the manager. He comes over and asks, "What's the problem?" You explain the situation to the manager who then explains to you that the waiter that served the couple across from you has been in the job a lot longer than the waiter who served you.

Your response is, you're in the same restaurant. You're paying the same price. You sat in the same area. They don't seem to be in a VIP area, so why do they seem to be getting VIP treatment?

The manager's response is "The waiter who served you has just begun. He's still getting his head around the requirements of the job." I don't know about you, but I wouldn't be very happy about this.

My response would be, "Well, if he's still in training, he shouldn't be on the shop floor serving customers until he understands the expected standard of delivery".

A simple system would avoid those issues and problems. Giving that waiter a simple checklist, a system, a minimum expected standard of delivery would ensure that all the guests in the restaurant receive the same standard of service regardless if you've been in that job for two decades, two years, or two weeks. It shouldn't matter. A systemised approach would prevent that from happening.

2. Standard procedures will make your business more efficient.

Having a standard procedure in place will save your business operations hours of time that are potentially lost, day in and day out. Think about how many tasks are involved in just one function of your business operations. If one basic job involves thirty steps, and in each one of those thirty steps, there are two or three considerations or decisions that need to be made, at each point the person doing the task has to stop and think, "Okay, what next? What do I need to do now?"

Every Second Counts

Even if it's only for a few seconds, when you add that up over the course of the day or a week and then a year, multiply that by each person on each job in each area of your business, those few seconds can soon add up to hours and days. A simple system removes the need to have to think, "What Next?" Because you know what's next. The system will show you or tell you what's next.

As human beings, we are fallible. We will make mistakes. We will forget. We will mess up. Those mistakes cost time and reduce efficiency. As we all know, time is our most valuable commodity. Once it's lost, it's lost, never to be regained again. By systemising your business, you're protecting your most valuable commodity, which will enable you to reinvest your time elsewhere.

Let me give you an example of how the absence of having a standard procedure in place cost me time.

I have been a podcaster since 2012. The process of planning, recording, editing and publishing a podcast contains many steps and stages and can be very time-consuming.

Planning, researching, recording, editing, mastering, formatting, publishing and promoting.

Without a standard procedure in place, I can't tell you how many hours I've wasted trying to complete each step by memory, but having to stop to remember what to do next. I would forget to do one step and move on to the next, before noticing and having to backtrack. I would do things in a different order or in the wrong order. This wastes a lot of time trying to remember the process and implement it in a correct way.

It's not that I didn't know what I was doing. It's that I was trying to execute the process by memory each time I carried out the task. Every time I went through the process, I would think to myself, "I should write this down or record this and capture it on a screencast."

I'm glad to say I've since learned from my mistakes and have now not only documented and systemised my podcasting process, but I've delegated that task so someone else can do it for me to the same standard as what I would've done myself.

3. Standard procedures will maintain quality standards.

By having standard procedures, you'll be able to maintain the quality standards of the service you offer. You don't want the quality of the experience your customers have to be dependent on how a person feels on any given day. You don't want to be dependent on how you feel when you're operating your business when it comes to maintaining those standards.

Regardless of the type of business you run and the products and services you deliver, you can't afford to risk being feeling dependant. You want to be able to guarantee your quality standards. You want to be able to deliver on your brand promise. If your brand promises a high-quality service, you want to be able to guarantee that that will be delivered to every single customer every single time regardless of who is delivering the service.

Data Make You Greater

It is important that you have the appropriate data at hand to be able to measure how your business is performing. This data could include how many of your website visitors convert to paying customers or how many of your current clients have purchased multiple products from you. It could be operational data such as the average time it takes to pick, prepare and pack an order.

Without a standard procedure in place, you will never truly be able to accurately monitor and evaluate how well you are performing. This is because tasks will be done differently by individual team members, so you will never have a concrete reference point to measure business performance against.

Having a standard procedure in place will give you more accurate data to monitor and evaluate what works, what doesn't work, and why. You'll be able to look at specific areas of the process and make small tweaks and changes to improve the process where required. You'll be able to identify bottlenecks and points of friction that slow down output or extend production time.

You'll be able to identify and remove unnecessary steps or stages in the process you have in place.

Ultimately, you'll be able to optimize the system making your business better, faster and more efficient.

You'll be able to do split tests to measure the progress of what you do. (I explain split tests in more detail in chapter 15 - Breaking the System.) Having a standard procedure in your business will help your team members and employees to operate effectively.

4. Standard procedures will ensure that clear expectations are set.

Manager Tools, a popular leadership and management blog and podcast, uses a phrase which really resonated with me when I was working in senior management in my corporate job. That phrase was: "In the absence of rules, people will make their own." I say the same with procedures. "In the absence of procedures, people will make their own."

We've previously discussed how this can cause problems with inconsistencies, inefficiencies, mixed quality standards, and so on. Here is an example of when I neglected to put clear procedures in place and the problems that the absence of procedures caused.

In my youth engagement agency, part of our work includes collecting data for the projects we deliver to our clients. This data usually includes the number of sessions we deliver, the number of young people we engage with and the demographics of those young people, such as age, gender, geographical areas. We also capture any positive outcomes that took place during each session as well as any issues raised by the staff or by the young people.

This data is be collected during every session and fed into our management information system. This allows us to provide our clients with a detailed project report at the end of each quarter and a final project report.

Here's Where Things Went Wrong.

I had made it clear to our staff that we need to collect this data every session, but what I didn't do was give them clear instructions on how to submit the data. At the end of the first quarter, it was time for me to get the report collated. I allocated about 2 hours to complete the report, which needed to be submitted in a few days. I logged into our management information system to pull down the data required. When I saw the data, I was mortified!

It was a complete mess!

There was no consistency with how the data was collected or collated. Each member of the staff had used their own style in recording the data. Some had used full names of areas and locations, other had used abbreviations.

Some had included age ranges of the groups of young people (e.g. 13 to 16 years old), others had left out the age of each individual young person. Some had included a detailed note summary of each session, others had put a few lines.

This caused me to have to do some additional work in deciphering the data and trying to make sense of it all. I was making numerous phone calls to my staff, asking them to help me to understand what they had recorded and what some of the data meant. This caused an inconvenience and frustration for both myself and the staff members. I finally got my head around the data and was able to produce a report that I felt was appropriate to submit.

As you can imagine, I wasted no time developing and implementing a standard procedure to ensure that the session data was captured in a consistent way. This was achieved by developing a simple spreadsheet template as well as examples of good practice that the staff could refer to.

Having a standard procedure in place for your business team to follow will ensure that everybody knows what is expected of them, everybody knows how jobs should be done, what the expected standard of delivery is, the expected time frames related to those jobs, and so on. A business team that is clear on what is required of them will usually operate much more effectively than a team of employees who have no clear direction.

A happy business team is an effective business team. A happy workforce is a productive workforce. Having a standard procedure in place will help to maintain a positive working environment where everyone is clear on what is required of them.

5. Standard Procedures will ensure there is business continuation.

Standard procedures will ensure that workforce production will not be affected by fluctuation in staffing levels, which is vital for small business sustainability and survival.

If one of your team members couldn't attend work for any reason or left the business, having standard procedures in place will make it much easier for someone else to come in and pick up that specific role almost immediately, and with very little training required. Whether that be another existing team member or a new employee who has recently joined the team.

Make Or Break

Having procedures in place for each role and each job function should enable anybody to come in, pick up and follow that procedure, and complete that task to the same standard as someone who has been doing it for years. Business continuation can be the life or death of a small business. It can mean make or break when it comes to certain client and contractual obligations.

Imagine, you promise your client that you will deliver their product or service by an agreed time. You then get a phone call saying that one of your main team members has reported in sick and won't be able to attend work for the remainder of the week. It could take you weeks to go and recruit and retrain somebody else to fill that position, which would mean that it is likely you will miss the agreed delivery date. You are left at the mercy of your client who could potentially cancel their contracts and never work with you again.

With standard procedures in place, someone else can come in and carry out that task, ensuring that the operations continue. The production line doesn't stop, and there is no disruption in service delivery. Your clients may never know anything had ever happened.

Even if the client is aware of the changes that took place in your business, they would potentially hold you in higher regard because you were still able to deliver the product and service as promised.

6. Standard procedures will give you a much better opportunity to sell the business in the future.

Many small business entrepreneurs never think they will eventually sell their business. They see their business as their baby. It's something that they will run for the rest of their lives. As a result of this thinking, they don't build their business as though they are going to sell it. They run it and work in it.

What Would You Want To See?

As a small business entrepreneur, take a step back and look at your business as if it was a business that you were going to buy. If you were buying a business what you want to see? If you were going to invest ten thousand pounds in buying a business, you would do your due diligence. You would want to see the books. You'd want to see the accounts. You'd want to see the standard procedures to get an understanding of how the business works.

You must approach your own business in the same way whether you're considering selling it or not.

Because you are investing your time, your energy, and your resources into building your business you should want to make it as valuable as possible. Don't make the mistake of failing to develop and implement standard procedures for all your basic business functions.

We've explored why you should systemise your business. Next, we're going to explore what you should systemise in your business. We'll focus on some basic business functions.

Questions:

Answer these questions in simple terms;

Explain how your business works.

Explain how you get new business leads.

Explain the process you have in place to convert those new leads into paying clients.

Explain the process of how you fulfill your clients expectations.

Explain your process for ensuring that your clients stay with you and become loyal customers.

Explain the process you have in place to move your clients through the sales funnel

What is your standard procedure to ensure that your existing clients refer you to other people, thus bringing in new potential clients?

To access the worksheet related to this chapter visit: www. tonylbrown.com/spbookbonus.

"Profitability comes from productivity, efficiency, management, austerity, and the way you manage your business."

— Carlos Slim

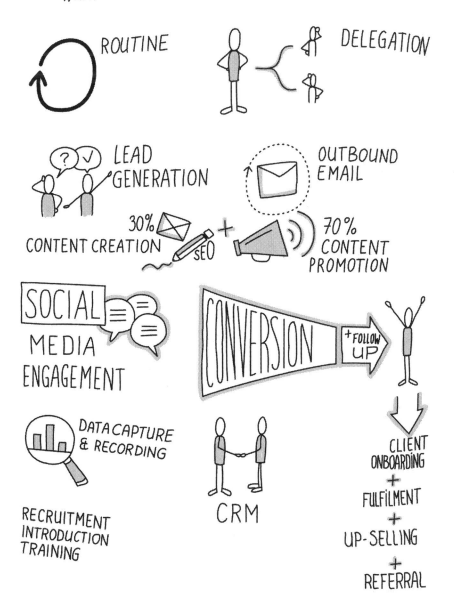

Chapter 7

WHAT BUSINESS OPERATIONS SHOULD HAVE STANDARD PROCEDURES?

In the last chapter, we explored why you should have a standard procedure to govern your business. In this chapter, we will focus on what you should systemise. This is a question I get very often when I first engage with a new client. Small business entrepreneurs often tell me, "There are so many different functions in my business, and so much activity, Where do I start?"

In this chapter, I will answer the questions:

What is the first thing you should systemise?

How do I start the process of developing a standard procedure?

Where Do I Start?

My initial response to the main question of "Where do I start?" is twofold. Firstly, you should document any business function you do on a continual basis. That is any task, any process, any function that you do on a regular and continual basis that turns the cogs in the wheels of your business. Secondly, you should have a standard procedure for anything you plan to delegate or allocate to somebody else. When I'm asked this question by my coaching clients, I flip it around and ask them, "You tell me. 'What should you systemise? What tasks do you do on a regular basis that makes your business turn?' Those are the things you should be systemising."

There's also the bigger picture, which we discussed in the last chapter, about viewing your business from a standpoint or a perspective of someone who is going to buy your business and what would they want to see. Ultimately, they'd want to see everything. The bigger picture is you would want to ultimately document your system and process for every business function you have.

In this chapter, I'm going to talk you through a few key business functions that I recommend you develop a standard procedure for as soon as possible. These business functions are applicable to any and every business regardless of your industry, your target market, the age or the size of the business.

Recruitment

The first standard procedure I'd like to suggest you put in place is in relation to the recruitment, induction, and training of your staff. Building your staff team is a core part of the development, growth and success of your business.

In a small business, your employees are your most important and probably your most expensive asset. Employing the right people for your business might be the most important activity you do.

You can have a fantastic product and a great marketing strategy, but if you have the wrong people trying to execute it, then things will break down. Recruiting staff is also a very costly exercise, both in terms of time and money. Your standard procedure should help you reduce staff turnover.

When you choose the right people for the job, train them well and treat them well, these people not only produce great results but also tend to stay with the organisation longer.

Without a standard procedure for recruitment, your business will struggle to find and keep the right people for your team. It's important to ensure that your recruitment procedure is supported by the core values and principles that your business is built on.

By having a standard procedure for recruitment, induction and training, you will ensure that the process is consistent. Now for some of you reading this, you might be thinking it's a little obvious. However, you'd be surprised at how many small-to-medium businesses and even a number of funded startups neglect to have a documented procedure for recruitment of staff.

You must be very clear about your recruitment process before you even consider interviewing anybody. Have a clear process about how you plan to identify potential new recruits, how you're going to have them express an interest in your job vacancies.

Here Are Some Questions You Must Answer:

What is your process for shortlisting the candidates and what's your process for interviewing and assessing those candidates?

Once they've been through the interview and assessment process, what's the next step?

What is your process for informing the unsuccessful candidates and for engaging with the successful candidates?

What are the key steps and stages in relation to inducting and on-boarding that new recruit?

What is the essential training they would need to undertake during their induction period?

Appropriate interview questions, ability tests and background checks help ensure that you employ a candidate who is suitable for the role and who fits the culture of the company. Your standard procedure should outline all the qualifications and abilities required to fulfill the role successfully, both essential and desirable skills. Without a standard recruitment procedure, you could end up with a poor performing employee who happened to slip through the net and this can be fatal for a small business.

Lead Generation

BusinessDictionary.com defines Lead Generation as:

"Process of collecting names and contact information about qualified [business] prospects which will be contacted by the salesperson for generating orders. ..."

What Is A Lead?

A lead is a person who has in some way, shape or form expressed interest in your company's products or services. They would have attributes that match those of your ideal client, the perfect person your products or services are developed for.

When I refer to lead generation, I'm referring to the ongoing activity you do in your business to raise awareness of your brand, to raise awareness of your products and services. The activities you do to put yourself in front of new and potential clients and customers. The activities you do to ensure that your business and your brand are visible to your target market.

Effective Lead Generation activities include:

Direct Mail

Networking

Blogging/Podcasting

Video Marketing

Social Media posting

Publishing a book

Public Speaking

Training events/seminars

Effective Advertising

Referral Systems

Public Relations and Publicity

Special Events and Promotions

Brochures and Corporate Literature

Email and printed Newsletters

Leaflet Drops or Inserts

Exhibitions and Trade Shows

In section two, I will walk you through a detailed step-by-step process of how to create your standard procedures. For now, that could be making phone calls to prospective clients, and you have a simple process in place where you identify those prospective clients and ensure that they are a suitable match for the products and services you offer.

You may have a process of doing some background research to equip you with some information before you make the phone call. You might have a script that you have at hand which you will follow when making the phone call, or a specific structure for responding to objections and answering questions that are raised.

Once you can identify the lead generation activities you currently do, and the ones that you aren't currently doing but should be, you can then go through the process of documenting the steps you must take to execute those activities effectively every time.

When documented, those steps and stages will become your lead generation standard procedure.

Questions:

What activities do you currently do to raise awareness of your business/products and services?

What other activities could you do to raise awareness of your business/products and services?

What activities do you do to put yourself in front of new and potential clients and customers?

What activities do you do to ensure that your business remains visible to your target market?

Content Creation

As this topic is pretty hot right now in the online marketing world, I'm going to park here for a bit longer than I will with the other points, so stick with me.

The phone is an effective way of reaching out to prospective clients, second only to face-to-face communication. Email marketing, a digital version of the tried-and-tested direct mail approach, is also very effective at reaching potential clients.

Content marketing, however, has also proven to be extremely effective in generating new leads and putting your products and services in front of your target market.

Get Found - Inbound

The difference with taking a content marketing approach is that where phone calls and email are outbound marketing channels, meaning a message is sent out from the business to the prospective clients, content marketing turns the tables and creates an inbound marketing channel. This means that the business puts out a piece of valuable content that the prospective client is drawn to out of interest and then a relationship is nurtured.

One of your prospective clients is looking for a solution to a problem they have. Their first port of call is to do a Google search. They type in "how to XYZ ..."

Think Like A User

If I want to find something out, learn something, review something, or validate something, I will jump on Google and do a search for it. Google presents me with a list of relevant search results, usually hundreds of thousands of results in response to my search. As I've learnt to trust Google's search results, I very rarely scroll past the first page of results. I click on one of the links on the first page of Google, which takes me to an article which is a blog post on a company's website. That blog post provides me with a direct answer to my problem. It's as if the article was intentionally written to answer my question.

That did not happen by mistake. That's because the author of the article (the content creator) understands content marketing, and how people like me and you use search engines. They know that their content can be served up to their target audience if it answers the questions their target audience are asking on Google. The also understand that if their content is engaging and informative, people will share it among their networks.

How does this look in practice? You've clicked a link and been taken to an article which answers all of your questions. It has informative and interesting advice, solutions and options. It even has links to other articles to answer any other questions you might have.

That article is found on the website of a company that provides products and services related to your search query. You are now aware of that company because of your search. They gave you something useful for free, and you now have a higher level of trust in the company because they helped you out.

Choosing Your Content Type

The type of content you choose to create will come down to what best suits the needs and the wants of your target market and the products and services you offer.

You could provide written content through a blog post, or audio content with a podcast. With YouTube you could create video content on your branded channel. You can live stream via Periscope, Blab or Facebook Live. With visual content you could make use of the many photo-sharing platforms such as Instagram or Flickr. Infographics and slideshow presentations also prove to be value forms of content.

Whatever you choose is up to you. However, you should have a standard procedure which would provide templates, guideline and quality standards to ensure you and your team produce great content for your target market.

This would include:

A content creation calendar or a production schedule, so everyone knows when content is due to go out.

A standard for how that content should be created and formatted. In the case of a blog post, a standard for headlines and subject lines.

A standard for how the content should be written, whether it be conversational or academic.

A standard for how your content should be laid out and formatted in the blog post.

A standard for how images should be incorporated and other relevant and appropriate media should be embedded, how links should be incorporated and so on.

I'm sure you can see the benefits and value of using content marketing in your business.

If you're not using content marketing currently in your business, then you need to. If you're not creating informative, interesting, relevant, actionable content for your target market, then you're at risk of becoming extinct in this digital age we are living in. You're at risk of having those businesses that do use content marketing leaving you way behind.

Having standard procedures in place will help you to consistently create high-quality content for your target market.

Content Promotion

Following on from content creation, you should have a standard procedure for content promotion. You've invested valuable time and effort in creating and producing content for your target market. The mistake many small business entrepreneurs make is that they leave it there. They produce the content, hit the publish button, and hope for the best.

However, the smart marketer understands the 70:30 rule. The 70:30 rule is a ratio for how much time you should spend promoting your content in relation to how much time you spend creating your content. Thirty percent of the time should be spent creating. Seventy percent of the time should be spent promoting.

I shared this ratio with a fellow entrepreneur, and their response to me was,

"I can't see myself spending a week promoting my blog post."

Yet, when we explored a little deeper and we looked at all the things they do once they've hit the publish button on their content and all the things they should do but they don't necessarily do intentionally, they realised that the 70:30 ratio was pretty accurate.

It's Pointless if Nobody Knows About It.

No matter how good your content is, if nobody knows about it and if nobody can find it, then it's good for nothing. If you've invested your time creating it, you want to invest three times that amount of time promoting it. You need a standard procedure to help ensure you promote your content effectively.

Using the example of a written blog post, you may author that post yourself or you may create the bulk of the written content and have a content writer polish it up for you and get it ready for publishing. Once it's published, I recommend that be the end of your role in that content. You should hand that over to a team member or a virtual assistant to do the rest, because your time is better spent creating content, not promoting it.

The team member you delegate that task to should have a standard procedure that will talk them through all the steps and stages of promoting that content. It should tell them what activities they should carry out to get the maximum exposure on that piece of content. This would include the social media platforms to post it on and how to structure those social media posts. How images should be used and the standard format for those images. The best sites to social bookmark that content to get maximum exposure. Who they should reach out to and the script to use when reaching out to individuals who would help promote that content.

Lead Conversion

Lead Conversion is the process of convincing a prospective customer to take the desired action based on your marketing efforts. In other words, conversion is simply getting someone to respond to your call-to-action.

Getting someone to sign up for you email newsletter is a conversion. Having them engage with the marketing messages you send them is a conversion. And, of course, buying your product or service is the ultimate conversion.

Ready For The Response?

So, you've rolled out your lead generation strategy. Phone calls have been taking place, outbound emails have been generating some activity. Your content creation and promotion activities are producing good results and you've been getting a lot of engagements on social media. The question to ask yourself is, "What happens when all those people come knocking?" It's very easy in the day and age we live in to get on social media, to jump on e-mail and to start making some noise. But then what?

When they come knocking, are you ready for them. Have you got a standard procedure in place to respond to the flood of inquiries that could potentially come as a result of your lead generation activity.

A standard procedure I recommend you get in place is your follow-up process.Through all your lead generation activity, you may get no response, you may get a warm response, you may get a hot response. Whatever the result is, you must have a standard procedure for following up. You need to have that standard procedure documented that anyone and everyone on the team know that this is what we do next.

"If this happens, then we do this."

That could be some template emails. It could be a script if it's a phone call. It could be directing them into a screening questionnaire. It could be directly arranging an appointment or sending a price list for products and services.

Whatever the appropriate next step would be, you have to have that documented so that everybody knows this is what you do next. Standard procedure!

Data Capture And Recording

You need to have a standard procedure in place explaining what data you want to capture and how it should be recorded. Leaving it up to each individual team member to make the decision about what information they will capture and record will cause you no end of frustration and lost leads.

When a team member has someone on the phone who is ready to buy your products or services, but then they don't capture the appropriate data or record it in the appropriate way it will have a negative impact on your sales performance

Having a standard procedure will help to ensure that everyone is clear about the information they need to capture and how and where to record that information.

Customer Relationship Management (CRM)

Customer relationship management, or CRM, is a core part of any successful business.

Yet, I'm surprised at how many small businesses don't have a standard procedure for CRM, (myself included at the time of writing this).

I underestimated the power of a CRM when I first started my business. I would keep the information here and there in my email clients, on my phone, and in Evernote. It was all a little scrappy. However, once I implemented a standard procedure for my CRM activities, it made monitoring and assessing information related to clients, both existing and potential, much easier.

It all came down to a lack of discipline. If everyone can get into the habit of recording and capturing data on a specific CRM platform, you will find monitoring and assessing that data much easier.

Client On-Boarding Process

Now that you have converted your potential client into an existing client, the next standard procedure you need to have in place is your client on-boarding process. That is the process your new clients go through to make their induction into your service seamless, painless, enjoyable and even remarkable.

Once your client has hit the buy-now button or they have agreed to buy your products and services, to sign up to your membership group, to sign up for your coaching program, what happens next? What are the steps you want to take them through to make that process seamless, painless, enjoyable and remarkable?

Take Them By The Hand

Your new customer has just given you some money in exchange for a promise you made them. That promise could be a solution to a problem, a benefit or a result. It could be the delivery of a specific product. Whatever the exchange, the customer needs to be taken through a process that will reassure them that they have made the right decision and that you will honor your side of the deal.

For example, you could create a series of short videos or an audio program that would guide your clients through that journey. It could be a series of emails that they receive during that induction period or that on-boarding period or it could simply be a frequently-asked-questions page.

Whatever is appropriate for your business and your clients, create a standard procedure to ensure that every client experience is consistent. This will ensure that their on-boarding experience is seamless, painless, enjoyable and remarkable.

There will be a number of questions that they will have that you need to answer.

You can develop a standard procedure that will take them by the hand and walk them through a series of steps that provides them the information and instructions that will make them feel reassured about their buying decision.

You want your new clients to say, "Wow, that was a great experience." You can create that "wow factor" through this on-boarding standard procedure.

Client Fulfilment Process

Once your new client is on board, the next system process you need to consider is your client fulfilment process. How are you going to deliver your value proposition? How can you ensure that the service or product that they signed up for is delivered to the highest standard and ensure that it meets or exceeds your customer's expectations?

Your standard procedure should lay out how your value proposition is delivered and ensure that it's not left down to how you feel at the time, and there is no room for misinterpretation when it comes to delivering your products and services to your clients.

Things That Make You Go WOW!

You want to ensure that when delivering your value proposition, you have built into that process the wow factor. What can you do to make your clients go, "Wow, that was remarkable I didn't expect that"?

The mistake a lot of small business owners make is that they think once they've got their clients on board, that's it, the job's done, the hard work is over. However, that's where it just begins. You now need to fulfil that client's expectations and deliver your value proposition, and you need to have a standard procedure in place for how you do that.

Large franchise chains are great at this. Take McDonald's for example. Whether you go to a McDonald's restaurant in your local city or you go to one in another country, it is likely the service you receive will be very similar. Your welcome greeting may be in a different language, but when translated, it will mean the same thing "Welcome to McDonald's, can I take your order please." The menu could be written in a language you can't understand, but you will be familiar with the items on offer. Your packaging will be the same and so on. The key word is consistency. Now it's unlikely you'll get the "Wow Factor" at a McDonald's restaurant, but what you will get is exactly what you expect from dining at McDonald's. That's because they specialise in having standard procedures.

Up-Selling

Once you've delivered your value proposition, you would want to keep moving your client through your sales funnel. If you're not familiar with the term up-selling, I'm referring to a process of encouraging your existing clients to buy more of your products and service. This could be higher or lower price point products or services that you offer. Having an up-sell standard procedure makes this process more efficient. When done right, up-selling builds a deeper relationship with your customers. Up-Selling is also easier than selling to new customers, because your current customers have already given you money and have had experience of doing business with you.

Learn From The Best

Amazon is the master of the up-sell and has embedded this standard procedure into their entire platform. I'm sure you've seen the "Other people who bought this also bought" - "Recommended for you" links while browsing on the platform.

Your up-sell procedure should guide your existing customers and clients through a journey where they would see their need for more of your products and services' or make a natural progression into your higher price point products and services.

The online printer service VistaPrint is relentless with their up-sell standard procedure and somewhat bullish in my opinion. Once you've hit the buy-now button and you proceed to the checkout, you have to run the gauntlet of multiple additional offers, upgrades, time limited offers and discounted second purchases.

You shouldn't be trying to force a sale on your customers. Your standard procedure will take your clients on a journey where they would see it's a natural progression. For them to continue on that journey, it would be beneficial for them to buy those other products and services or invest in your higher price products and services.

I know the example of Apple products is over-used. However, I think it's a good example when it comes to up-selling. Think about the journey from iPod to iPhone to iPad to MacBook to iMac and so on. I'm sure you can see the principle. For some of Apple's customers, it actually works the other way around. There were some Mac users who went on to buy a MacBook laptop and then decided to get themselves an iPhone and an iPad and so on.

Referring back to the McDonald's example—Have you ever been asked if you want to "Go Large"? That's classic up-selling in action. And that cashier will ask every single customer they serve. Every single time. Why? It's Standard Procedure!

Having a standard procedure in place for up-selling is extremely beneficial for your business and will have a significant impact on your profits year after year.

Referral Process

Many small business entrepreneurs make the mistake of leaving the choice of referring their business to other potential clients in the hands of the existing customer. Having a standard procedure in place that will ensure that your existing customers and clients refer your business to their friends, to their family, to their colleagues and generally to others will produce a much higher rate of referral.

Now what that process would look like will come down to the type of clients and customers you serve. However, the key point is to have a system in place to ensure that referrals are made or at least requested.

Forcing The Referral

Obviously, you can't force a client to make a referral to somebody else, or can you?

I heard a story about Hotmail, the webmail company which was bought out by Microsoft some years ago. They saw a steady increase of users when they first launched. However, their explosive growth came when the CEO had the idea of placing a referral link at the bottom of every email that was sent through the Hotmail platform, and it simply read, "Click here to get your free Hotmail account". Every single email that was sent via the Hotmail platform had this referral link embedded in it, and the results speak for themselves.

The most effective referral programmes make the referral be in the customer's best interest. A number of online services give their users upgraded services for bringing new users to the platform. Dropbox, the cloud storage solution service, for example, gives you an additional 500mb of storage for every user you bring to the platform. Up to a maximum of 18GB. This is a great incentive, as you can never have enough online storage space.

Project management tool Trello gives you one free month (up to a maximum of 12 months) of their premium service Trello Gold for every user you bring to the platform.

Persistent Not Pushy

Your standard procedure should ensure that you earn the right to be referred. That your customers want to make the referral because it will benefit them in some way.

It should ask for and encourage the referral in a professional and appropriate way.

Your standard procedure should be persistent in asking for the referral. Not pushy or obnoxious, but persistent: e.g. a link at the bottom of every email, in every newsletter, on product packaging, on your website. Everywhere that is appropriate. Your standard procedure should make the process of making a referral quick and easy.

Now the type of business you run will influence the other standard procedures you would have in place. I have given you an overview of some of the core procedures every business should have in place. It's not an exhaustive list, but it will give you something to consider.

To access the worksheet related to this chapter visit: www. tonylbrown.com/spbookbonus.

"In the short term, most things that contribute to productivity growth are very painful."

— Janet Yellen

OBJECTIONS AND EXCUSES

MY CLIENTS HAVE HIRED ME TO ...
You set the expectation!

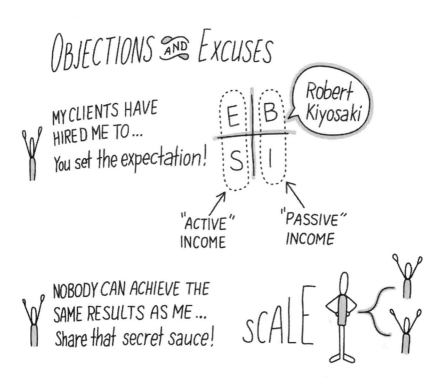

"ACTIVE" INCOME

"PASSIVE" INCOME

NOBODY CAN ACHIEVE THE SAME RESULTS AS ME ...
Share that secret sauce!

SCALE

HOW DO I MAINTAIN OR ASSURE THE QUALITY OF SERVICE ...
Have a standard operating procedure!

FRAMEWORK FOR CREATIVITY

I FEEL LIKE I HAVE TO BE THERE TO OVERSEE THE WORK ...
Train your staff!

Chapter 8

OBJECTIONS AND EXCUSES

This topic comes from a recent initial consultation I had with a prospective client. During what I call a discovery session, we were exploring this individual's current position, and it came to light they recognised that they would benefit from reducing the amount of time they currently spend working in their business. When I say working in their business, I mean specifically delivering their core service to the client.

They had developed a personal brand, a consultancy and a speaking service which also included coaching and mentoring. Much of that was based on them delivering it directly to the client, or to the end user. It was all about them going out, securing the contracts, getting the work, and then going out and personally delivering on those contracts.

I was talking to this individual about my experience. I could relate to where they were because I'd been there myself. I was using my experience to show them how they could also make the transition from working in their business to freeing up more time to be able to spend developing and growing the business. I could hear the frustration from this person and I knew exactly where they were. It was like they were stuck in this place where they couldn't let go.

What I want to really focus on is some of the excuses that I've heard. I say excuses respectfully. You can call them excuses, you can call them objections. Essentially, these are the reasons, the excuses, the objections that I've heard from solopreneurs as to why they are resistant to delegate work to others and are still working in their business.

My Clients Hire Me

This is the most popular reason people give as to why they can't delegate their work. The mindset is this:

"My clients have hired me to deliver this piece of work. My clients have bought into my personal brand. They've bought into my services, so I must deliver on this. My clients want me to turn up and deliver this work."

My response to this is that you've created this situation. You have trained your clients to expect to receive the service directly from you. This is a typical business model for someone who started as a freelancer, or a consultant. I can relate so much to this because that's how I started. I was in that positions. It comes from reproducing your former corporate gig, but as a freelancer.

I know it's a bit of a sweeping statement, and it's not the case in every single scenario, however, when you track the journey of the person who is in that position, they have recreated their corporate job, but as a freelancer.

Don't Become The Product

Simply put, they're working for themselves, and they've made themselves the product.

You are the product, you are the service. Your skills and experience, your approach, your methodology, your practice, you're bringing all this to the table, and you're offering you as the product or service. You've got these skills. You understand this problem. These are your solutions. It all comes down to you.

I was in that position. I went out, and I wanted to get work. It was all based on my experience, my skills, my track record at my corporate gig. I sold myself as a freelancer. It was great for a season because I felt like I was working for myself. I'd gone out there, and I'd proved that I can go this alone. I can do it myself. I don't need a corporation behind me. I can go out there and get work for myself, and it felt great. In reality, it was very limited. I was very, very conscious of this. If you're in this position, you'll be aware of it as well.

The Cashflow Quadrant

Let's look at an example using the *Cashflow Quadrant* by Robert Kiyosaki. If you've ever read *Rich Dad, Poor Dad,* then you know what I'm talking about. Robert Kiyosaki has created what he calls the Cashflow quadrant. It's a diagram with four squares, and each square represents a position or a model as to how you generate an income. The first one is E for employee.

The second one is SE for self-employed. The third one is B for business owner. The fourth one is I for investor. If you search for "Cashflow Quadrant" in Google, you'll be able to look into it further.

Essentially the ideal position is not to remain in E as an employee, and SE which is self employed, because, in the self-employed quadrant, you are still employed. You're still an employee, you're working for yourself. If you stop working then you stop getting paid.

The Walk Up Call

This is where lots of freelancers, consultants, and solopreneurs are. They're stuck in the Self-Employed (SE) quadrant. They've got a job. They work for themselves.

This is very limiting because you can't scale yourself as a self-employee. You can only be in one place at one time. Although you may feel like you have escaped the rat race, and made the transition into the business world, you're still trapped as you haven't necessarily got a business. I know this is a bit of a sobering wake up call when it's put so bluntly, because internally you feel like you have got a business because you work for yourself. But ask yourself this question;

If you were to stop working, and you didn't go and deliver on a contract, or you didn't turn up and do that coaching or mentoring session, would you still get paid?

The likelihood is that you would default on that contract. So, in all reality, you don't have a business. You own a job.

Nobody Can Achieve The Same Results As Me.

When I hear this objection, I laugh to myself, because I've been there. I've said the same thing and had the same hang ups, or the same mindset as this. Only I can achieve these results. Only I can deliver to this standard. Only I can make the impact that my clients want to see, or that my value proposition promises.

It may be true that we all have our own personal approach, our own style, our own skills and experience that we bring to the table. No one can necessarily do what you do, how you do it. However, that doesn't mean that nobody else can achieve the same results as you.

Share The Secret Sauce

My main response to this is, if you're planning on running your own business, you have to create systems and processes to enable others to achieve the same results as you. It's the only way. If you plan to remain as a freelance consultant, and trade time for money, then that's fine. If you want to have a business that runs without you necessarily having to turn up everyday, and deliver, then you're going to have to share the secret sauce, as it were. You're going to have to share the ingredients of the secret recipe that allows you to achieve those results. Sticking with the recipe ingredients analogy, unless you want to be stuck in a kitchen all day, you better share those ingredients. You better share that secret sauce.

I said to the individual that I was having the discovery session with, "You don't see Richard Branson driving any trains, or flying any planes, unless it's a PR related stunt." You need to break out of that scarcity mindset, because it is small minded thinking. It's limited to think that no one else can achieve the results that you can achieve.

Some Questions I Ask My Clients Are:

How are you going to scale the business?

How are you going to create some longevity, or legacy within your business?

What's going to happen when you want a break, when you want to go on holiday?

What's going to happen?

You Used To Be A Trainee

You've got to be able to pass down that skill, that knowledge, and that methodology to somebody. You're going to need an apprentice one day." Also to the individual, I said, "Somebody gave you your first break. There was a time where we were all trainees, and somebody gave us a break. Somebody gave us an opportunity. Somebody took us under their wing, and taught us the skills that we have, that we use today."

You must avoid small-minded thinking and be willing to create systems and processes to enable others to achieve the results that you can achieve. It's the only way you're going to be able to scale your business.

How Do I Maintain, Or Assure The Quality Of The Service?

This follows on from the previous excuse, or objection. It's when the individual believes that only they can deliver a quality service. They are fearful that if they entrust another person to work on their behalf, the quality will be compromised. I can relate to this, and it's a degree of perfectionism that kicks in. It has to be delivered like this, in this way, or else it's just not gonna be as good as what I can achieve.

However, this is where your systems and processes come into play. It all comes down to having a standard operating procedure, or SOPs as they are called. You want to know how to maintain the quality of the service: Develop a set of standard operating procedures.

Equip Your Team For Success

These could consist of templates, worksheets, scripts, outlines, checklists. If it's a case of doing presentations, then provide the slides and the speaker notes that go along with those presentations. If it's a case of doing some mentoring, or coaching, then provide the framework and some training that goes along with the service. Then, within that you can create a set of quality standards to ensure that anyone you delegate to knows that this is the expectation.

It's your job to equip your team with everything they need to enable them to operate at the expected standard.

There may be a service, or element of service, that you deliver that would benefit from having your staff personalise, or deliver in their own unique way. You want to allow for that. You don't want to make it so rigid that it robs them of their personality, or their unique style of delivery. Ultimately, they're going to bring something new to the table. They're going to bring something unique to the table that you're going to want to take advantage of and benefit from.

Minimum Standard Requirements

To allow that to happen you could develop and implement some minimum standard requirements. What that means is that you're creating a framework that your staff should work within.

This still allows room for their creativity, and for their personalisation. But it is within a framework. As long as all the work meets this set criteria every time it is delivered, you can do what you want within that space. So you're not stifling the person delivering on your behalf. You're allowing them to be themselves, and to be creative, and to personalise and deliver in a unique style. You're ensuring that at a minimum, these processes are accurately being followed. Yes, you can maintain and assure the quality standards of your service without you necessarily having to be there.

I Feel Like I Have To Be There To Oversee The Work.

I might as well deliver it myself. I feel like I have to be there to oversee and monitor the work being delivered, so I may as well deliver it myself. The truth is, this may be a reality, and this may be required for the first few times you allocate, or delegate the work to somebody else.

Maybe during an induction period, or an on-boarding period, you will have to be present. You will have to oversee the work, and ensure that the individual whom you've delegated the tasks to is competent, that they understand that task, that they do it right, and that they do it to the expected standards.

Focus On The Long-Term Benefits

When you're investing that time, it might seem like it's a waste of time and it's a waste of money, because you might be thinking to yourself, well I'm paying this person to be here to free me up from having to be here. However, I'm here as well delivering, or overseeing the work they're delivering. So then it's costing you twice as much, because you're paying them, and you're also investing your own time. You could have delivered it yourself.

I understand that, however my response is, "It is short term." It is only for a specific period of time. If you think mid- or long-term, then you can see the benefits of that. You may invest two or three hours of your time to train that member of staff, and to ensure that they understand what's required of them.

That two or three hours, even if it was two or three days, that short period of time is going to free you up from delivering that piece of work forever. It's definitely a worthwhile return on investment.

If you keep the long-term benefit in mind, it helps to justify the investment. You might spend a whole session alongside a member of the staff, or a whole working day overseeing them, and being on hand to guide them. That investment is going to free you up for good to allow you to focus your time, and energies on other things. Eventually you're going to have to trust somebody to deliver that work on your behalf, or else you're going to be stuck delivering forever. It's not scalable.

Invest some time and energy in training your staff, and demonstrate to them the expected standard. Then let them get on with it.

Although you may have objections to delegating your work to others, and those objections may be genuine and valid, by implementing a standard procedure to underpin your delegation, you can confidently remove yourself from delivering the day-to-day work of your business, and focus on investing your time in the improvement and growth of your business or simply doing "other things" you choose to do.

If you've had or expressed any of those objections, then I trust that this chapter has helped you to overcome them and ultimately free yourself from that trap.

Time For Some Action

Your time and energy and efforts are better spent developing, building and growing your business. Unless you want to be stuck delivering the service directly for the lifetime of your business, then I really encourage you to take action.

This doesn't mean you can never deliver the service again at a time that you choose to deliver. It just means you do it when you choose to. Reflect on some of the objections, and even if it's only on a small scale, bit by bit, step-by-step, start to implement a standard procedure, and take yourself out of the business.

I guarantee you, you will not regret it. The first time I made that transition, the feeling was fantastic. That feeling of; I don't need to turn up. I don't need to deliver, and I'm still getting paid. This is fantastic.

What that allowed me to do was to focus on identifying more clients, developing more programs, more products, more services. If you think every time you go, and deliver a service face-to-face, or directly, your business is on hold, because your time is taken up delivering rather than developing and growing,

I encourage you to make the transition. Put some of these steps in place. Develop and implement your standard procedure.

In the next section, we're going to focus on the how, and we're going to look at a step-by-step process on how you can begin to create a standard procedure for your business.

To access the worksheet related to this chapter visit: www. tonylbrown.com/spbookbonus.

"Productivity is never an accident.

It is always the result of a commitment to excellence, intelligent planning, and focused effort."

— Paul J. Meyer

SECTION II

HOW TO CREATE YOUR STANDARD PROCEDURES - A STEP-BY-STEP PROCESS.

In the previous section, we explored why you should systemise, and what you should systemise. In this section, we will focus on how to systemise your business.

I've told you why, I've told you what, now In this next section, I'm going to tell you HOW!

I'm about to take you through a step-by-step process of how to create a standard procedure to enable you to systemise your business, reduce your workload, be more productive, and ultimately, be more profitable.

Let's Go!

"You only have control over three things in your life—the thoughts you think, the images you visualise, & the actions you take."

— Jack Canfield

STEP 1 CONCEPTUALISE YOUR SYSTEM

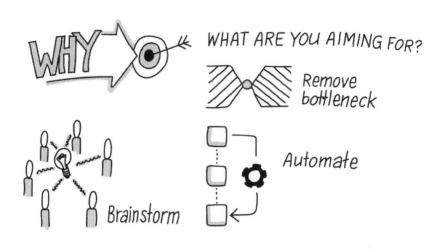

WHAT ARE YOU AIMING FOR?

Remove bottleneck

Brainstorm

Automate

REMEMBER OPTIMIZATION IS NOT JUST ABOUT SPEED AND COST, BUT ALSO ABOUT QUALITY, CONSISTENCY, AND USER EXPERIENCE.

WHAT WORKS
AND WHY

WHAT DOESN'T
AND WHY

WHAT WILL AN OPTIMIZED SYSTEM LOOK LIKE?
AND WHY

DESIGN THE OPTIMAL, ULTIMATE SYSTEM & PROCESS. THEN, DETERMINE THE CLOSEST YOU CAN GET.

CONCEPTUALISE YOUR SYSTEMS

The first step is to conceptualise your systems. In the simplest of terms, when I'm talking about conceptualising, I'm referring to simply understanding what you want to achieve with your standard procedure, and how it might look once it's completed. It's about drilling down to a specific system that you've identified that you want to develop, and understanding why you're developing it and what you want it to do.

At this point, we're not really focused on the nuts and bolts of how the system is going to work. In this first step, we're just focusing on why are you developing this system, this specific system. There are a few reasons why you would develop a specific system. Are you looking to speed up a process? In every business function, there are processes that you follow to make that business function happen. Whether they're documented or not, they exist. When you're about to go through the process of documenting those standard procedures, ideally you want to aim to optimise them at the same time.

Why Are You Developing This System?

Are you aiming to speed up a process or reduce friction? Meaning to make your workflow more streamlined and time efficient? There may be steps and stages within a specific system that you could remove or tweak slightly which could significantly speed up the process and remove any friction points that are slowing it down.

Maybe you want to remove a bottleneck in the process. There could be a specific point where the process is hindered or slowed down because it's waiting for a specific response from somebody, or waiting for a necessary document or element of the product to be provided, and it's creating a bottleneck. You're developing this system to remove that bottleneck.

Maybe you've got an existing manual system that you want to automate. Maybe you want to reduce or replace the existing manual dependency. Maybe you want to enhance the user experience, and by systemising this specific function, it can add a quicker, better experience to the user.

At this stage of the process, it's all about brainstorming. It's about getting everybody around the table who is involved in this business function at every touch point around a table and finding out how they would see this system working, and not only working but working at an optimised level.

Optimising The User Experience

I'm conscious that when I say optimised, quite often the entrepreneur's mind thinks about speed, you think about getting things done quickly, and at the lowest cost to the business. However, it's always important to remember that it's about ensuring that quality standards are maintained, that there is consistency across the brand, and that the user experience is what's being optimised.

When I say user experience, that could be internally, regarding the person that is going to be running that system and working that process day in and day out. Also, the end user who potentially could be the customer or the client who will benefit from having that system in place.

At this stage, you want to give everybody who is involved in this business function an opportunity to contribute their opinion. If it's an internal system that will only be used by employees, team members, etc., then you would have a brainstorming session focused on capturing all their thoughts, their ideas, in relation to the system and process you're looking to develop. You'd want to find out what are the frustrations they have with that process currently, and if they could optimise this in any way, what would they do?

As the CEO of the company, you are the person with the final say on the standard procedure that will be implemented. However, you also need to remember that you're not necessarily the person who's going to be using and implementing your standard procedure on a day-to-day basis, so it's very important that you get input from the individuals who are going to be using your standard procedure. You want to get as much information and insight from them as possible.

You may see some bottlenecks from your position. However, because they are the ones on the ground using your standard procedure, or implementing them on a day-to-day basis, they're going to have a different perspective. They're going to see things that you can't see. They're going to understand what slows these systems down, what slows the process down. They're going to be able to have a better understanding from a ground level as to when bottlenecks are caused and why they're caused. It's your role to create an environment where they feel that they're able to share, very openly and honestly, their thoughts and feelings about the current processes and procedures that are in place. At this stage, it's your job to listen.

Exercise:

Identify the business function that you're going to focus on, and invite everybody who is involved or contributes to that business function to attend this workshop. Have Post-It notes, pens, flip charts, flip chart paper and markers available to capture thoughts, ideas, opinions, throughout the session.

One of the first questions you need to ask is this;

"Assessing This Current Business Function, What's Working And Why?"

Encourage everybody to contribute. Capture all the responses on the flip charts, and encourage team members to capture their own thoughts on Post-It notes and place them on the flip charts.

Once you've exhausted all the responses, move on to the next question, which is;

"What's Not Working And Why?"

With both of these exercises, make sure you focus on finding the why. From experience, it's very easy to allow team members and employees to share what's not working, but neglect to really explore and understand why is it not working. That's where the gold is. It's in the why.

If it comes to light that a specific stage or step is a problem or a bottleneck in the process, don't move on to another point until you have been able to identify, validate and understand why it's a problem, what's the bottleneck, what's the issue, who does it affect, and how does it affect them. What's the impact?

Summarise And Seek Solutions

Once you've exhausted all the responses here, have the flip charts and Post-It notes displayed around the room, so that everyone can see them, and summarise the key points on one or two specific sheets or flip charts, or on a whiteboard. The next thing you want to do is to move on to potential solutions. So you've looked at what's working and why. You've also looked at what's not working and why. Now it's time to explore what will an optimised system look like.

In this stage, you want to lift the limits and allow everybody to think big, to get creative, and even have a little fun.

I like to ask the question:

"If You Had Access To Unlimited Resources, What Would Your System And Process Look Like?"

Let's create the ultimate system. This may seem a little childish or foolish to some. However, the idea here is to get the creative juices flowing and allow your team to let loose and to open up, so you can really hear what they would like to happen. What would the ideal system look like? If you're developing a system that is focused on the end user, or your customers and clients, then you would do the same with them. You may have a focus group where you invite them along and allow them to contribute to a similar workshop.

Regardless of who you're working with, you want to really encourage them to think big, get creative, don't allow the current limitations, the current barriers, to hinder your thinking. The idea here is we want to design the optimal, ultimate system and process.

Back Down to Earth

Once you have captured all the ideas and concepts that would make up your optimal system, it's now time to come back down to earth and to analyse the optimal system that you've created from a realistic point of view, and ask yourself the question:

"Based on our current access to resources, based on the current reality we're operating in, what's the closest we can get to this optimal system?"

Once you have documented that system, you're ready to move on to the next step. You've got a basic concept. You understand what you want to achieve with a documented system. You understand why you're developing this system. You've explored what an all-singing, all-dancing, ultimate system would look like, and you have outlined what that system would look like based on your current access to resources. It's now time to start doing some research. That's what we're going to look at in the next chapter.

To access the worksheet related to this chapter visit: www.tonylbrown.com/spbookbonus.

"Don't reinvent the wheel, just realign it."

— Anthony J. D'Angelo"

STEP 2 DOES THE SYSTEM ALREADY EXIST

COLLECT ALL AVAILABLE INFO

COMPARE TO AND SEARCH FOR SIMILAR SYSTEMS

REVERSE ENGINEER

REMIX! DON'T COPY

ASK

PEOPLE WILL TELL YOU WHAT THEY NEED, IF YOU ASK

DOES THE SYSTEM ALREADY EXIST?

I n the last chapter, we explored the idea of conceptualisation in understanding what you want to achieve from developing your specific systems. You used a process of capturing thoughts, ideas, suggestions and solutions from everybody involved in that system. The next step in the process is for you to begin to do some research with the aim of finding out if a similar system or process already exists.

Now as I've alluded to a number of times previously, many of the standard procedures you'll be documenting already exist because you already do them on a day-to-day basis. The issue is that often they're not documented. In this research stage, you're finding out, exploring and identifying any existing documentation related to the system and process you're developing. You want to capture as much information as possible related to that system. You may find that you have notes, check sheets, things to do lists that all relate to steps, stages and phases within that process.

The system you're documenting might be something that already exists internally and you're just updating it. Get as much documentation related to the existing system as you can get your hands on. Your goal is to begin to create a file that contains anything related to this system or process.

There Is Nothing New Under The Sun

Once you've looked internally, you need to turn your attention outside of your current business. You want to explore and find out, "Does a similar system exist externally?" At the time of writing this book, it is early 2016, and we are very much entrenched in the information age. Information and knowledge are easily accessible as never before. Within a few seconds, you can have access to a wealth of information on almost any given topic in the palm of your hand via your smartphone. When you're developing your standard procedure you need to make the best use of the access to information you have.

Regardless of the type of business you run, I guarantee you that if you search long and hard enough, you will find a system somewhere that is similar to the system you are aiming to develop, or, at least, has elements of the system you aim to develop. You don't need to create your system from scratch, or, at least, you shouldn't have to. There will be something you can model it on. There will be an existing system somewhere that you can emulate and use elements of to help you to develop your procedures. You don't need to reinvent the wheel. There's a verse in the Bible that says, "There is nothing new under the sun," and how true this is today.

This Is The Remix

In my younger days, I was involved in the music industry as a DJ and a producer. There was a saying in the production circle that "Everything is a remix." What that saying meant was that everybody pulls inspiration from other places. Though you may be creating a unique piece of music, you've been inspired by another piece of music, either consciously or subconsciously. What you're creating is a remix of the other pieces of music you have heard.

This same theory can be related to the development of a standard procedure in your business. Regardless of which business function you focus on, there's something out there that will, at least, give you a framework or a starting point to help you to develop your system.

For example, if you're developing a lead generation process which would involve an email marketing campaign, then a quick hack would be to sign up for a number of email marketing campaigns from competitors and other people who you believe would have a system in place that you may want to emulate.

Once you've signed up for that process, observe and assess each step and stage involved. What was their landing page like? What was the text on the landing page? What was the call to action? What was their opt-in sequence like? How was the first message structured? What was the core content? and so on.

When you've been through a few of these processes, you can begin to reverse engineer the system which would allow you to understand it much more. The main aim here is not to copy what other people are doing, but to understand the what and why behind what they do to give yourself a framework to develop your own standard procedure.

Remixing Is Not Copying

By no means do I endorse the copying of other people's material. However, if someone's got a good system in place, then I don't see any harm in emulating that system and ensuring that your system is just as good. Another suggestion i make to all my clients is to read blog posts and articles, watch videos, and listen to podcasts related to the topic or theme for which they're developing a system. Whether that be sales, lead generation, content creation, content marketing or recruitment, whatever it may be, there is a ton of content at our fingertips that will give you some real insights and information related to that subject. Much of that information has been condensed down and is very easy to consume. I encourage all of my clients to make the best use of the content that is available. Not just the content alone, but also the comments and forum threads that may come from those articles.

The Voice Of The People

You would be surprised how much you can learn about the wants and needs of certain specific customer segments, user groups and niches while reading blog comments and forum threads. They will tell you exactly what people like, what they don't like, and how they want things to work. You can even go in there and post your own question, or start your own thread to get the specific information you need, which you can then implement into the development process of your own systems.

You will hear individuals complaining about the sign-up process for a specific service, or raving about how great the on-boarding process was for a new service they signed up for. You have the opportunity to jump in there and ask further questions. What was so great about it? What made it outstanding for you? If you could improve it in any way, what would you do? What would you have changed, and so on?

You can even take to social media and ask the questions, "What would the ideal ... process look like to you? When signing up for a new service, what are the most important things for you?" You can also make use of customer surveys using tools such as Google Forms, Survey Monkey, Typeform and others, and reach out to your existing clients or customers.

If it's an internal system, contact your staff and ask them the specific questions you want answered. The main thing at this stage is to get as much information as you can which will arm you once you start to create your standard procedure.

Once you have completed your research and you have all the relevant data you need to help you better understand the direction you should go with your standard procedure, then you're ready to move on to the next stage where you'll begin to start the initial development process of your standard procedure.

To access the worksheet related to this chapter visit: www. tonylbrown.com/spbookbonus.

"The journey of a thousand miles begins with a single step."

— Lao Tzu

STEP 3 CAPTURE THE SPECIFIC STEPS

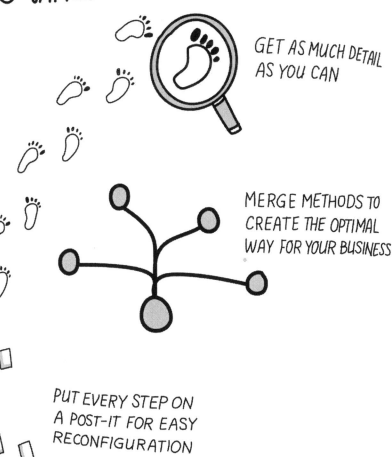

GET AS MUCH DETAIL AS YOU CAN

MERGE METHODS TO CREATE THE OPTIMAL WAY FOR YOUR BUSINESS

PUT EVERY STEP ON A POST-IT FOR EASY RECONFIGURATION

CAPTURE THE SPECIFIC STEPS

You should already have a good idea or, at least, a basic outline or framework to start this next process. This is where you begin to capture all the steps and stages involved in the standard procedure you're developing.

This is one of my favourite stages in this process, because this is where we begin to identify all the little unseen, undocumented, but extremely important steps within a process that are quite often taken for granted.

When a person has done a job for a specific period of time, there are elements of that job that they will do spontaneously without even thinking about it. There are decisions that they will take, and observations they will make whilst carry out that task that wouldn't register as being significant enough to document. However, it's those little unseen and undocumented steps that quite often make the way for the person to do that job effectively and which produce the desired results.

Let's Get Into The Details

You've got your outline and you know what system you're developing. Now it's time to brainstorm. It's back to the whiteboard, the flip chart, and the Post-It notes and pens. The aim of this step is to capture everything. You want to include everyone who has ever done this specific task or job that you're documenting. Start at the beginning and take a slow walk all the way through the process from start to finish.

Be a bulldog with this process! In fact, no, I've got a beagle, so be a hound dog. You want to sniff out every single step, stage, action, spontaneous, subconscious reaction and get it all down on paper.

One tip when you're doing this process is you can also use an audio recorder either on your smartphone or on a dictaphone or other audio recording device, and record the discussion with your team about the process, which you can later refer back to in the next stage. The idea here is to dump it all down. Get as much detail as you can. Don't worry too much about the logical order because that might hinder or delay the flow of this activity. Just get the information down.

As an example, here's my podcast production process. You can see how many steps are involved.

The podcast production recording process:

Confirm episode topic

Create outline for that topic in workflowy.com or Evernote

Outline three to five main discussion points

Add three to five sub-points under each main discussion point

Research additional information

Open audio recording software

Run a test recording and adjust the mic, position, and levels accordingly.

Record episode

Save raw audio files

Place raw audio file in shared Dropbox folder

Edit and Master episode

Format audio file

Include podcast artwork

Upload all mp3 files to media host

Create episode blog post

Produce show notes

Create episode feature image

Proofread post

Publish

Once the episode is published, I then trigger the podcast promotion process, which has it's only checklist.

Your Way May Not Be Best Way.

It's important to remember that each individual will have a different way of achieving the same result. That's fine. It's your job as the CEO of your company to create the optimal way.

What's the best way to achieve the desired results?

What's the quickest and most efficient way?

Which method will achieve the desired results and give the end user the best results or the best experience?

It's also important to accept that your way may not necessarily be the best way. That's why it's important to have everybody involved in the process. You may have members of the staff who have worked on this job for ten years and you may have an apprentice who's been on the job for less than six months. Each of them will make a valid contribution to developing the optimal procedure. Don't dismiss anybody's contributions, even if they are not necessarily in line with your own personal method or approach. At this stage, it's about capturing all the steps involved in completing the task.

When doing this exercise, I've found that writing each step down on an individual Post-It note is one of the best ways because this allows you to move them around and replace them during the next stage of the process. If you just write a long list on a sheet of paper, you're going to struggle to create a logical order later on.

Get yourself a few pads of Post-It notes and only write one step per note. To speed up the process in preparation for the next stage, you could begin to categorize the steps, but don't get too consumed with trying to map it out in a logical order, as that's what we're going to do in the next stage.

To access the worksheet related to this chapter visit: www. tonylbrown.com/spbookbonus.

"Creating a company, is like baking a cake. You have to have all the ingredients in the right proportion."

— Elon Musk

^{STEP} 4 CREATE THE BLUEPRINT

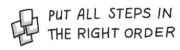 PUT ALL STEPS IN THE RIGHT ORDER

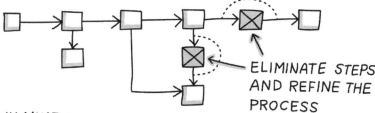

ELIMINATE STEPS AND REFINE THE PROCESS

KEEP IN MIND :

IF {THIS} THEN {THAT}

REPEAT UNTIL DONE
(FOR NOW)

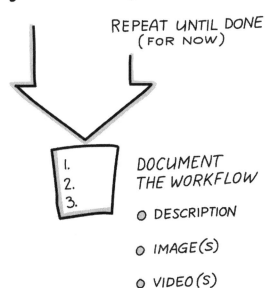

1.
2.
3.

DOCUMENT THE WORKFLOW

o DESCRIPTION

o IMAGE(S)

o VIDEO(S)

CREATING THE BLUEPRINT

I n the previous step, you went through the process of capturing all the steps and stages involved in your standard procedure. Now it's time to start putting all those steps and stages together into a logical order and create your standard procedure blueprint. If you followed the process I suggested and used Post-It notes to capture all your steps and stages, it's now time to lay them all out and organise them in the sequence in which they will run, starting at the beginning and working right the way through to completion. You're mapping out the chain of events and sequence of tasks that would need to be executed for this job to be completed successfully and to the required standard.

Time To Refine

It's also at this stage that you would begin to eliminate any unnecessary steps and refine the process. I would recommend at this stage that you still have everybody involved in the process contribute to this exercise. There may be some steps that you feel are necessary. However, others may be more hands-on and much closer to the task will put forth a good argument as to why a certain step or stage could be removed. It's also during this stage that you'd begin to identify the possible tools and resources required to achieve the desired outcome.

As you work through the logical order of the sequence, ask the questions:

- Is this step a necessary requirement for this task to be completed?

- Is this step only achievable by manual input?

- Can this step be automated?

- What tools and resources could we make use of to do this step or stage quicker, better, more efficiently?"

Once you've answered all those questions and you've identified the potential tools and resources you will use, it's time to link all the components together. At this stage you should still be working on a flip chart or a whiteboard. Remember, we're still mapping out and creating the blueprint.

IFTTT

When going through this process, one of the main questions or statements you want to bear in mind is: "If this, then that."

As you work through the sequence, ask yourself the questions:

"If this happens, then what should happen next?

When this task is complete, then this happens, so what should happen next?"

If you are working with a current system that you're trying to improve, ask yourself what currently happens, and then ask the question: "What do we want to happen?"

The aim here is to create an efficient, optimised system. Something that is fit for its purpose. You may want to work through this process a few times, working from start to finish in one sweep, and then going back to the beginning and working through it again until you feel that the system you have developed is, as they say, the one.

Document The Workflow

Once you've completed that initial exercise and you have your Post-it notes all laid out in a logical sequence, and you've identified your tools and resources that you're going to be using to make the system click together, it's now time to document the workflow. This is where you begin to transform what you have laid out on your whiteboard or on your flip charts into a document.

There are a number of tools and resources you can use to document your workflow, many of them online tools and many of them are free. Initially, you could use a basic Word document, or if you're familiar with using mind mapping software then I would recommend that you use a mind mapping tool such as Simple Mind or Mind Node.

There are many other free mind mapping apps that you could use to do this. I would also recommend using a tool like Evernote and make use of the checkbox function to create a checklist.

This can also be done in an Excel or Google spreadsheet. As long as you can document the workflow at this stage, the tool doesn't matter.

At the time of writing this book, I have recently started to use Process Street, which is a simple, free and powerful way to manage your team's recurring checklists and procedures. They also have business and enterprise accounts which you can pay for to benefit from a number of features and functions, but even with the free plan you can create your process templates, you can run multiple instances of that template as a checklist, and assign those checklists to team members and track their progress as they work through them.

Process Street has a very simple and clean interface which makes it very easy to use. It also has a library of pre-populated templates that you can use or amend to best suit your needs.

Easy Access is Essential

Regardless of the tool you choose to use and whichever method you choose to document your workflow, make sure that it's in a place that is easily accessible for everyone who will be running that task and using or following that workflow. Again, Google Drive, Dropbox and Evernote are all useful cloud-based tools that allow for easy sharing and online access.

Also make sure that your tool can be easily amended and updated without too much effort. In addition, you want to be able to include hyperlinks the other resources that would add further instruction, clarity, and even training on each point, or any necessary points, within the workflow.

There may be a stage or step in the process that requires a little bit more detail or explanation for it to be achieved to the required standard. Rather than leaving it to interpretation, you would add a hyperlink next to that point or step that would link to those additional details. That could simply be a Word document or a text note. It could link to an article somewhere online. It could link to another website or webpage, or it could link to an audio file or even a training video showing your team member exactly what they need to do to hit the expected standards.

Give Them Everything They Need, And More.

In my workflows, I almost always link to a video screencast that I've created specifically for that step in the process. I've also linked out to other videos on YouTube that would give further instruction on the task. And I've linked out to blog articles that I've found useful, and even podcasts that I recommend the team member listen to if need be to give them more information and insight about the specific step or stage they're working on.

The aim is to give them everything they need, and more, to be able to ensure they can complete that task without having to come back to you and ask questions. There's no shortage of information out there. There's no shortage of instructional articles, videos, ebooks, and other resources that offer extremely valuable hints, tips, hacks, and tutorials on how to do almost anything. Make the best use of them. Now you've mapped out your blueprint. It's time to move on to the next stage. This is where you're going to create your first prototype.

To access the worksheet related to this chapter visit: www. tonylbrown.com/spbookbonus.

Standard Procedure

"I love taking an idea from prototype and then to a product that millions of people use."

— Susan Wojcicki

STEP 5 THE PROTOTYPE

 BLUEPRINT → **TEST** and simplify

 ☐ RUN IT AS DOCUMENTED

 ☐ WITH THE ACTUAL TOOLS

 ☐ BY THE ACTUAL PEOPLE

 ☐ MEASURE TURNAROUND & TASK TIME

 ☐ ANALYSE EFFECTIVENESS & EFFICIENCY

STEP 5

THE PROTOTYPE

Now that you've mapped out your blueprint and put all your steps together in a logical sequence, and documented the workflow. In this step, you're going to create and test your first prototype of the system. This is a step where you pull it all together, set up all the tools and templates, and test the system. This is the step where we begin to see the system in action. This is where we begin to see the theory in practice.

Your standard procedure could include the use of a number of different tools and applications, which need to be integrated into your system. This will mean you may need to sign up for accounts, register with services and download any relevant applications. You'll then need to set these up so that they function correctly when using your system.

These could include:

Project management software such as Basecamp, Asana, or Trello

Online communication tools such as Slack or Skype

Email autoresponders such as Aweber, MailChimp, or

GetResponse

Web-based cloud storage solutions such as Dropbox or Google Drive

Online scheduling tools such as Calendly, Acuity Scheduling or Apointy

Online survey software such as Google Forms, SurveyMonkey and Typeform

Any other necessary software, tools, or resources required.

The great thing about the day and age we live in is that there are many free tools available to do more or less anything you need to do.

A Word Of Warning.

Don't get too consumed with trying to identify the perfect tool. When you first set up your system, just use whatever you feel most comfortable using and whatever does the job.

When I first developed my client screening and scheduling system for my coaching services, I used a simple Google form to create the client screening questionnaire. Although I felt the form was a bit clunky and didn't look very nice, it did the job. As time went on, I tried a few different tools and ended up sticking with Typeform, from typeform.com, which I still use to this day because it is slick and simple to use and looks great.

Keep It Simple

Something else to be aware of is the overuse of online tools and applications, as this can create additional hoops to jump through and also increase the possibility of errors within a system.

An example of this was with the recruitment process for our youth engagement agency.

The initial process worked like this:

Candidate to go to webpage

Candidate to add email address to email capture box (Aweber)

Candidate to check your inbox for confirmation message

Candidate to confirm email address

Candidate to check your inbox again

Candidate receives a link via email to expression of interest form (Survey Monkey)

Candidate to complete expression of interest form

Team member to manually check Survey Monkey for completed from

Team member to send follow up / confirmation email

In the initial process, what I wanted to do was capture the email addresses of everyone who expressed an interest in joining the agency. Because I already had an account established with an email autoresponder service, AWeber.com, I wanted to build the list using that software. I felt that this would also give me an opportunity to filter out people who weren't serious or filter out any spammers as they would have to go through a double opt-in process of signing up through AWeber, confirming their email, and then would receive a link via email to complete an online application form, which we had set up in SurveyMonkey.

As time went on, I noticed that there were a number of people who had expressed an interest and signed up through the initial opt-in process but never went on to complete the online application form. I also noticed that I never used the email opt-in list which I was building in AWeber, so I made a decision to cut the AWeber signup step out of the system completely.

The new updated procedure has been significantly streamlined:

Candidate to go to webpage

Click "I'm Interested" button

Candidate to complete expression of interest form (Typeform)

We receive an auto-notification with form data.

Candidate receives auto notification with confirming receipt and details of next steps

Test The System.

One of the main activities in this step is to test the system to see if it really works as you thought it would have worked on paper. I don't recommend rolling the system out publicly at this stage. If it's a system for external use, you may want to do some internal testing with team members.

Testing your standard procedure is a crucial step before it goes live. It is important that you find and fix any major flaws in the systems at this early stage, rather than when your business operations are dependent on them and they fail.

Refer to the example I shared about our expression of interest system for new recruits. If it's an internal workflow, then get one or two team members to run the system.

The main thing you want to focus on is "Can they complete the entire process from start to finish without having to ask for any additional support or input from anybody else, and complete the task to the required standard?" If the answer is yes, then you've successfully developed a workable system.

I always suggest running it a few times through, and where there is the possibility for variables, try to run it taking all those things into consideration. This could include the person running the workflow. It could be the time of day that the task is being carried out. Or it could be the general nature of the task. Either way, you want to take all the variables into account when testing the system.

You would also want to record and measure some specific outcomes. For example:

The turnaround time from start to finish.

How long does it take to run the task?

The effectiveness of the system.

How effective is it?

How efficient is it?

Does it do what you want it to do?

Is it producing the same standard of output every time?

Once you're confident that the system is able to be run by someone other than yourself, allowing them to deliver the required standard of output every single time in a time frame that you're happy with, then you're ready to move on to the next step, which is to launch the system.

To access the worksheet related to this chapter visit: www. tonylbrown.com/spbookbonus.

"The best entrepreneurship happens in low-stakes environments where no one is paying attention, like Mark Zuckerberg's dorm room at Harvard."

— Eric Ries

STEP 6 LAUNCH THE SYSTEM

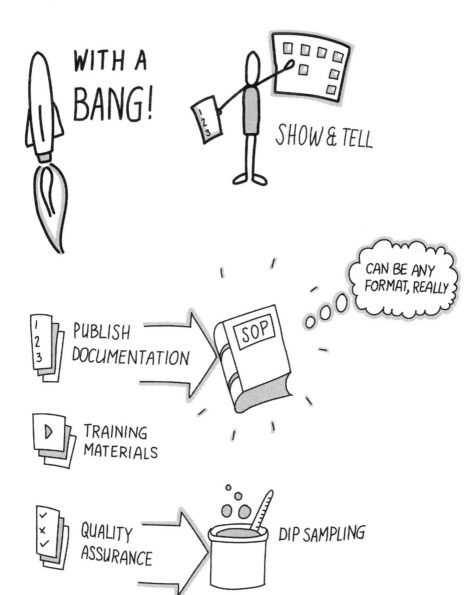

WITH A BANG!

SHOW & TELL

PUBLISH DOCUMENTATION

SOP

CAN BE ANY FORMAT, REALLY

TRAINING MATERIALS

QUALITY ASSURANCE

DIP SAMPLING

LAUNCH THE SYSTEM

After a successful prototype phase, you are now ready to launch the system. This is where you stop doing things the way you used to do them and implement the new system you have recently developed. This is where you make the commitment to the system.

Launch Party

In launching a system, I recommend you make a pretty big deal about it in the same way as you would launch a new product or service, as you're going to want everybody on the team to know the new system is in place. It's out with the old and in with the new. Everybody in the organisation needs to be aware of that. You want to remove every possible excuse for a team member to say they didn't know, so launch your system with a bang. Announce it in your staff newsletter. Even have a grand launch event. - Alright, maybe don't go that far.

The main thing is to make everybody aware that the new system is in place. You will need to publish the documentation that has been created, including any workflows, flowcharts, descriptions and diagrams related to the new system. You're going to add the new system to your standard operating procedure manual. That manual could be a printed physical 3-ring binder or folder. It could be a series of electronic documents such as PDFs or Word documents. It could be a series of webpages that your staff have access to or a shared Dropbox or Google Drive folder containing all your standard procedure. This standard operating procedure is going to be the manual that governs how your business operates.

Show, Tell, Teach

You will need to create some training materials to go alongside your documented procedure. This could include an initial introduction video or audio file talking a new member of the staff through the process. You can also include visual flowcharts, diagrams and infographics. Visuals work extremely well when it comes to workflows, as a lot of people learn better through visual communication. The art of communicating messages, ideas and information in a way that can be viewed and understood is very powerful.

When a visual message is used alongside text or speech, it has a greater power to inform, educate or persuade a person or audience than the written or spoken message alone. This is especially powerful in education and teaching. People learn best through seeing, hearing and doing.

When developing your standard procedure, use images, diagrams, screencasts, screenshots, annotation, links to other videos and so on. The aim is to produce something that someone who has never carried out the task before can pick up and successfully achieve the task to the required standard. There is no shortage of video tutorials on YouTube.

Here's One I made Earlier

If someone else has put something together, then use it. Also, give examples of what the finished product should look/sound/feel like. If you want image designing, then provide an example of a previous image that has been designed to the specification you want.

If you want podcast editing and mastering, then provide an example of an existing piece of audio that you want your podcast to sound like. This gives your team something to reach for, a point of reference, rather than feeling around in the dark hoping they hit the mark you expect. You've heard me mention that I use screencasts to walk my team through a process. This is becoming a standard procedure.

Screen Capture

I've mentioned, I'm also starting to use screen capture a lot more to provide quick unedited feedback on anything. Jing is a free screen capture app that lets you capture basic video, animation and still images, and share them on the web. Quicktime player also has screen capture capabilities.

I can hit a button in my taskbar and start recording my screen and my voice in a few seconds. This file can then be quickly saved and sent to a team member via Slack or Skype. It can be dropped in a shared folder and a link sent over to them, and they can be watching and hearing my feedback in a few minutes.

I have become aware that my preference for learning is to show and tell, which give me clear, concise and reinforced information. Don't tell me something - show me how.

You can have some posters printed and displayed in the working area of the people who will be working on this task. If your team is remote and work predominantly on computers, you could have them created and displayed as a screensaver or desktop wallpaper that can be referred to quickly and easily without having to search for an image or a file.

Quality Assuring Your Standard Procedure

Once your standard procedure is launched, you're also going to want to create a process for quality assuring the system. Having a thorough standard procedure is one thing, but ensuring that the people running the system follow the standard procedure step-by-step every time is another thing. You're going to need to develop a method of quality assuring the output of the work being delivered or carried out.

Dip Sampling

One effective way of doing quality assurance is to do what's called 'dip sampling'.

Dip sampling, also known as random sampling, is a method of randomly selecting a sample of a specific output and checking that the quality meets the required minimum quality standards. For example, let's say you're running an eCommerce business and you've launched an order picking, packing and delivery procedure.

For example, You could create a dip sample by randomly picking three or four packages off the end of the line throughout the day and checking to ensure that they have been picked, packed and prepared for delivery in line with the procedure.

This achieves a few things. Firstly, it reassures you as the business owner that the system is being followed and that your staff team are working in accordance with the new procedure. It also lets the staff team know that the system is important enough for you to check it and that you're serious about the new procedure. It also sends a message to the staff team that work can and will be checked at any given time to ensure that it meets the standard requirements. Nobody wants to get caught out slipping. I have gone as far as doing this with my company's social media posting. I created a minimum requirement for social media posts that go out on Twitter.

Taking Corrective Action

This may seem to some people a little overboard, but I guarantee this is the only way you're going to get things done in the way you require them to be done.

I think I'm very fair and understanding when it comes to minor errors and missing the mark occasionally. However, when I've addressed the matter of missing specific procedure points more than three times, this to me means more than manual error. There's either an issue of competence or a blatant disregard for the system that is in place.

As I've said previously, you're the boss; you're the business owner; you're the CEO of your company. It is your responsibility to ensure that quality standards are upheld. It's your job to ensure that the products and services that are being developed or delivered are to the highest standard and that your customer experience is over and above their expectations at every touch point and interaction with your business.

Now I'm not encouraging you to be a mean, callous, taskmaster of a boss. What I am saying is to manage your business appropriately. If that means making tough decisions, taking corrective action to ensure that standards are met and even dismissing people, then so be it.

Now your system is embedded and operational and producing great results. There's only one more thing for you to do. It's probably the last thing you would ever consider doing. That is to break the system. That's what we're going to discuss in the next chapter.

To access the worksheet related to this chapter visit: www. tonylbrown.com/spbookbonus.

"Without change, there is no innovation, creativity, or incentive for improvement. Those who initiate change will have a better opportunity to manage the change that is inevitable."

— William Pollard

STEP 7 BREAKING THE SYSTEM

 WHEN YOU'RE DONE BUILDING, START BREAKING THE SYSTEM

 SPLIT TESTING

 FOCUS GROUPS

 KEEP INNOVATING
instigate & embrace change

BREAKING THE SYSTEM

If you have read all the way through to this point in the book and followed through with the exercises in each chapter, then congratulations.

You have the done the hard work of creating your standard procedure which will enable you to reduce your workload, increase your productivity and ultimately increase profits. Now your standard procedure is running smoothly. You should therefore find you are spending less time working in your business and find you have more time to do other things.

The question you need to ask yourself now is what do you spend your time doing. In an earlier chapter, we spoke about your end goal, otherwise known as your *why*. That was the reason why you want to systemise your business, why you want to have more free and flexible time. If you've followed these steps, then you should find that achieving your end goal and realizing your *why* is a much closer reality than previously.

Staying In The Game

In chapter five we discussed the misconception of abdicating from your role. It's not a time to retire just yet, as you still have a very important role to play in ensuring that your standard procedure not only runs efficiently, but continues to improve on a regular basis. To secure the long-term success of your business, you're going to have to stay in the game and stay on top of things.

You may be asking the question: "My standard procedure is running efficiently and effectively, what else do I need to do? I've optimised my standard procedure and everything is running great. My employees are happy. My customers are happy. My suppliers are happy. I am happy. My work here is done."

Remember Blockbuster?

We live in a world of change, consistent and continual change. Trends are forever changing. Supply and demand are forever tipping back and forth. The wants and needs of customers in your marketplace will forever change. Tools and resources are changing every day. Manufacturing processes and business systems also need to change to stay relevant and to allow the business to be in a position to compete as an industry leader. You don't want to get left behind and you don't want to become irrelevant.

Blockbuster was a very successful brick-and-mortar video and DVD rental chain. For a time. The leadership and management team at Blockbuster neglected to keep its finger on the pulse of industry trends and stubbornly refused to move with the times. That made way for the new kid on the block, Netflix, to absolutely blow them one of the water. Blockbuster went into administration and ceased trading, and are now the example-of-choice when talking about a company that neglects to keep up with industry trends.. Netflix has now become a name synonymous with watching movies.

If It Ain't Broke, Break It!

Author, entrepreneur and marketing thought leader Seth Godin introduced me to the concept of 'Breaking the system'—and I love it! The old saying goes, "If it ain't broke, don't fix it." The new saying is "If you want to improve it, you have to be willing to break it." But what does that really mean? I'm sure you've seen or heard that quote being shared around social media ...

"If you always do what you've always done, you'll always get what you've always got."

I've seen this quote attributed to Henry Ford, Anthony Robbins, Mark Twain and others. I don't know who to credit, but nonetheless, the saying is true! My version of the saying goes like this ...

"If you want to see different results, do something different."

You will have invested a lot of time and energy in developing and implementing your system and it may be working well. However, once you have all your systems functioning and your business is ticking away nicely, your job as the CEO, founder, managing director, president or another title you choose to hold, is to improve each of those systems.

Your job is to break the system. It's all about growth, change and innovation. Try something different, switch things up, take some risks. There are a few ways you can do this:

A/B Split Testing

A/B split testing (also known as split testing or A/B testing) is a method of comparing two versions of a specific thing against each other to see which one performs better.

Split testing is mainly used in web design and online marketing activity as well as the web application and online software markets. The A and B refer to the two variants, which are the control and variation in the controlled experiment. As the name implies, two versions (A and B) are compared, which are identical except for one variation that might affect a user's behavior.

For example, a webpage has a "Buy Now" button for a product that is for sale. The variation for the split test could be that on page A the button is green and on page B the button is blue. Everything else remains exactly the same. The aim of the test is to see which colour button performs the best in converting sales.

Split testing is a great way of figuring out what works best with different user groups. These could include internal team members or external customers.

Here are a few ideas of how you could split test your standard procedure. You could run the following tests and measure the results:

Make changes to the workflow of one specific team member.

Change your method of communicating with a specific team member from written communication to exclusively using voice messages with them.

Change the method of task delegation with one specific team member.

Reduce the amount of time allocated to a regular task for one specific team member.

This is all about testing and optimising what works best and then implementing those results.

For more information on A/B split testing. You can find a link to it on the resources page for this book at www.tonylbrown.com/spbookbonus.

Focus Groups

A focus group is a small group of people, typically around eight in total, brought together to take part in a focused discussion, evaluation and assessment of a specific product or topic. The session is facilitated by a moderator who takes the group through a set series of questions or themes related to the topic.

Focus groups are another way of finding out how you can improve and optimise your systems. You can run a focus group session internally with your team members or with a group of people from your target market. This approach is great for encouraging and generating new ideas, however, the moderator (which will probably be you) must keep the session focused. One effective approach when facilitating a focus group is not to ask the questions ...

"How can we improve the system?" or "What changes can we make to the system?"

But better to ask ...

Here is step A in the process, what can we do to make it ... [insert the improvement you would like to see]?

This helps to maintain the focus of the specific options, rather than leaving it open. Even though your system may be working well currently, be sure that it can be improved or optimised. Don't be afraid to break the system. You don't want to end up like Blockbusters.

To access the worksheet related to this chapter visit: <u>www. tonylbrown.com/spbookbonus</u>.

CONCLUSION

I trust that as you have progressed through the chapters in his book, you have come to believe that it is possible for you to develop and implement a standard procedure that will allow you to systemise your business, reduce your workload, increase your productivity and increase your profitability. Ultimately giving you more free and flexible time to do the things that you want to do.

I'm sure that you also realise how much discipline and focus you will need to resist the temptation of doing the work in the business yourself, and to commit yourself to remain dedicated to your role as the CEO of your company.

I trust that the principles which I've shared, along with my own personal experiences will give you a good foundation on which your work of developing and implementing your standard procedure can be built.

Together, we have learnt that in order for you to scale your business you must free yourself from your business. The day-to-day operations of your business cannot be dependent on you being there to run it.

We discovered that your business is a series of systems, all working together to produce a specific product or service. That your role is to ensure that those systems are optimised and continually running as efficiently as possible.

We explored the concept of finding your *why*. And that it is extremely important to have a very clear reason as to why you're undertaking the process of creating your standard procedure.

We have overcome the misconception of abdicating from your role, and that having a standard procedure and moving away from the day-to-day operations of your business does not mean that you have no work to do. In fact, the opposite is true, and your standard procedure will allow you to focus more on your actual role and responsibilities as the CEO of your company.

We have established that without a standard procedure, the only two options you have to increase the amount of income you generate were one: work harder, faster and longer. Or two: charge more for the services you deliver.

We then explored some valid reasons for having a standard procedure to govern your business, such as consistency in the quality of products and services, more efficiency, the ability to monitor and evaluate effectiveness, set clear expectations and provide for business continuation.

We discussed some of the business operations that should have standard procedures underpinning them, such as lead generation and conversion, outbound email, content creation, content promotion, social media engagement and others.

We have also addressed the objections and excuses from solopreneurs as to why they are resistant to delegate work to others and are still working in their business. We established that an investment of time and energy in developing and implementing your standard procedure, and training others to follow it, is going to free you from having to do the work yourself and allow you to focus your time and energies on other things.

We have looked at the practical step-by-step development and implementation of a standard procedure, discussing the 7 steps involved, which are: 1. Conceptualise your system. 2. Does the system already exist? 3. Capture the specific steps. 4. Create the blueprint 5. The Prototype. 6. Launch the system and 7. Breaking the system.

This book was written to offer you a challenge, a map, and a foundation on which you can begin the process of creating your standard procedures. I hope that you and those around you will join me on this extraordinary journey of systemising your business, reducing your workload, increasing your productivity, and increasing your profitability. Giving you more free and flexible time to do the things that you want to do.

I wish you every success.

NOTES

Ch 1 – p. 11 - *Platform: Get Noticed in a Noisy World* by Michael Hyatt

Ch 1 - p. 11 - www.michaelhyatt.com

Ch 4 – p. 23 - *The E-Myth* by Michael E Gerber

Ch 4 – p. 24 - *Start with Why* by Simon Sinek

Ch 5 – p. 28 – Article "Sales Productivity Secret: Automation Isn't Enough" by Brandon Redlinger

Ch 5 - p. 29 - *Virtual Freedom* by Chris Ducker

Ch 7 – p.39 – BusinessDictionary.com

Ch 8 – p. 51 - *Cash Flow Quadrant* by Robert Kiyosaki

CH 8 - p. 51 - *Rich Dad, Poor Dad* by Robert Kiyosaki

NOW WHAT?

How Can I Help You Implement the Steps in this Book?

Hire Tony Brown As Your Business Systems Strategist

Tony is passionate about helping as many small business owners and entrepreneurs as possible experience the many benefits that come from developing and implementing a standard procedure in their business. Through his coaching services, Tony will support and guide you through the process of systemising your business, identifying and addressing your most immediate needs and then helping you to set goals. Holding you accountable in regular one-to-one coaching sessions to ensure you stay focused on achieving the results you want. Visit www.TonyLBrown.com/Products and book your initial consultation session to see if Tony can help you achieve your business goals.

Book Tony Brown As A Keynote Speaker/Trainer

Tony is a confident, inspiring and engaging conference speaker. By booking Tony to speak at your event, you will get a professional and competent communicator on subjects relevant to small business and entrepreneurship, such as business systemisation, productivity, reducing your workload, working remotely, managing a virtual team and Content Marketing.

Tony is also an accomplished training workshop facilitator, who enjoys nothing more than meeting with groups, other small business owners and entrepreneurs, and getting the post-it notes, flipchart paper and pens out, and having a solution-focused mastermind session. Visit www.TonyLBrown.com/speaking and check Tony's availability for your event.

Join The Onward Business Mastermind Community

The Onward Business Mastermind Community is a members-only community designed to give you the inspiration, training and resources you need to build, implement and improve your business. With access to our active online community, live monthly Q&A mastermind calls, expert advice, tutorials, interviews with entrepreneurial thought leaders, templates, check sheets and resources, you'll have everything you need to take your business to the next level. We only open registration twice a year. So if you're interested in joining the community, visit www.Onwardbmc.com to add your name to the waiting list, so you don't miss the next opportunity to join.

Listen To The Standard Procedure Podcast

Standard Procedure is my weekly podcast, where small business entrepreneurs can find practical, actionable and easy to consume information, advice, insights, resources and inspiration to help you develop systems, processes and strategies to reduce your workload, be more productive and gain more free and flexible time to do the things you want to do. By subscribing to the podcast, you will automatically get every episode for free as soon as they become available. The easiest way to access the shows is by using a podcast application on your iPhone or Android phone. These applications make discovering, subscribing and listening to podcasts so much easier. The biggest advantage is that you don't have to load iTunes on your computer, subscribe, and then manually sync to your phone. Visit www.tonylbrown.com/podcast or go to iTunes and search for Standard Procedure Tony L Brown.

Listen To The Business Systems Explored Podcast

Business Systems Explored is a weekly podcast that Tony co-hosts with Vinay Patankar, CEO of Process Street. They interview tech startup executives, entrepreneurs, marketers, and thought leaders to do a deep dive exploration of the mechanics behind their business.

Listen to hear cutting edge, practical information, insights, methods to help you build and refine your business systems. Visit www.BusinessSystemsExplored.com or go to iTunes and search for Business Systems Explored.

ABOUT TONY BROWN

Tony Brown is a Business Systems Strategist, Coach, Author, Speaker and Trainer. He also blogs and podcasts at TonyLBrown.com. Tony's goal is to help small business entrepreneurs to document and systemise their workflows, reduce their workload, increase their productivity and profitability. How? By helping them to create, implement and refine Standard Operating Procedures (SOPs).

Tony's corporate background is in local government senior management. Specifically in the youth and community sector. During the latter part of his "9 to 5," Tony was able to successfully lead and coach a team of around 30 staff members for over 5 years through a time of massive budget cuts, service restructures and job losses, working in a city made up of some of the most deprived communities in Europe. During this time he learnt a thing or two about problem solving, overcoming adversity and getting things done. The keys to his success were twofold: systemisation and equipping people.

In 2012 he began to intentionally work towards building his own business to a point where he was able to walk away from his corporate job and go full-time self-employed. In 2013 - one year later - he did just that. In addition, he was also able to employ a small team of staff to help scale the business. And he was able

203

to do all this in just 12 months. His youth engagement agency "Youth Work Toolbox LTD" now provides professional training and casual staffing to organisations who want to engage with young people effectively. He worked hard to achieve all of this while balancing a busy family life with his wife of 14 years, Nicola and their four children.

In Early 2014, Tony was invited to attend the UK Houses of Parliament to be a part of a Select Committee Panel to explore "How to Nurture and Develop Entrepreneurship and Enterprising Behaviour Amongst Young People." Now, Tony is on a mission to help other business owners and entrepreneurs to systemise their business operations and create more free and flexible time to spend with the ones they love the most.

An entrepreneur at heart, in 2015 Tony established "Onward" Business Mastermind Community. His aim is to create a community where like-minded entrepreneurs connect to plan and prepare for business success. Onward is made up of an exclusive weekly mastermind group, an online community and support forum and a series of live, in-person events. Tony's goal is to create the world's largest business mastermind community of over 1 million active members. Visit www.Onwardbmc.com for more information.

ONLINE SOFTWARE, TOOLS AND APPLICATIONS

Acuity Scheduling - Easy online appointment scheduling software.

Agile CRM - Contact management, marketing automation and social suite.

Allthings - Better management and distribution of work within a team.

Amazon S3 - Store and retrieve any amount of data, anytime, from anywhere.

AnyMeeting - Hold online meetings and webinars.

Appointlet - Enable your clients to book appointments right from your website.

Asana - An information manager for workspace. Organize people and tasks effectively.

AutoRemote - Control your phone remotely.

AWeber - Email marketing software and services.

Basecamp - Project management application.

Buffer - Autoschedule your social networks.

Campfire - Share files, images, code and more right within a chat window.

Capsule CRM - Keep track of your clients and prospects online.

Close.io - CRM to help you close more deals and make more sales.

Constant Contact - Reach, engage, and acquire new customers through email.

Contactually - Manage your contacts across email, social media and mobile.

ConvertKit - Email marketing platform for professional bloggers.

Dropbox - Store your files online, sync them to all your devices, and share them easily.

E-junkie - E-commerce solution for shopping carts and buy now buttons.

EmailONE - Email Marketing Platform that focuses first on freedom and security.

Evernote - Note taking application - Capture anything you need to remember.

Expensify - Import expenses directly from a credit card to quickly create reports.

GetResponse - Automated email newsletters, campaigns, online surveys.

Gmail - Free email service provided by Google.

Google Analytics - Industry standard web and mobile analytics package.

Google Calendar - Organise your schedule and share events with others.

Google Cloud Print - Send PDF documents or other text to a network printer.

Google Docs - Online word processor - create and format text documents.

Google Drive - Store files online and keep them synced with your devices.

Google Forms - Create, send and share online surveys.

Google Sheets - Online spreadsheets software.

Google Tasks - A simple task list. Works inside Gmail, Android, and Calendar.

GoToMeeting - Video conference software.

GoToTraining - Provide interactive training sessions, regardless of location.

GoToWebinar - Set up and deliver an online video and audio conference.

Gravity Forms - Wordpress plugin that makes it easy to create powerful forms.

Highrise - Manage contacts, schedule follow-ups, set reminders, and convert leads.

HootSuite - Social media dashboard.

Infusionsoft - All-in-one marketing and sales automation software for small businesses. Insightly - Manage customers, contacts, opportunities and projects.

Kanbanery - Online visual project management tool for personal or team use.

KanbanFlow - Lean project management tool.

KISSmetrics - Person-based analytics package - track events and funnels online.

LeadPages - Landing page generator with professional templates.

MailChimp - Email marketing service provider.

OmniFocus - Task management platform for Mac, iPad, and iPhone.

OneDrive - Store files online, edit Office documents in the free Office Web Apps.

OneNote - Sync your ideas, sketches and notes across all your devices.

PayPal - Send and receive money, make an online payment.

Pocket - Save articles, videos and links to view on any device.

Process Street - Document, track, automate and optimise processes.

Producteev - Organise tasks for your team in the simplest way.

QuickFile - UK based cloud accounting software.

RescueTime - Automatically log the time you spend on applications and websites.

Rev - Audio transcription service - from audio or video into text.

Salesforce - Customer relationship manager (CRM) application.

SalesforceIQ - CRM app that integrates with your team's email inboxes.

ScheduleOnce - End-to-end solution for scheduling with prospects and customers.

Slack - Team communication platform - instant messaging and document sharing.

Stripe - Accept payments online and in mobile apps.

SumoMe - Web traffic growth tool - email list builders, sharing buttons, and heat maps.

SurveyMonkey - Create online surveys.

Teamchat - Messaging platform for teams of unlimited size.

Trello - Team collaboration tool - organize everything to keep your projects on task.

Typeform - Create slick online surveys, questionnaires and forms.

Unbounce - Drag and drop to create landing pages in minutes.

Wistia - Professional video hosting services.

WordPress - Create a beautiful website or blog.

Wunderlist - Manage all your personal and professional to-dos.

Zapier - Integrate with hundreds of other apps to automate your work.

ACKNOWLEDGMENTS

I thank God for giving me another chance. Everyone deserves another chance. I was not looking for Him, but he found me in a very dark place and revealed His beautiful Son, Jesus Christ to me. Since then, everything has changed. And for that, I am eternally grateful.

This book is dedicated to my beautiful wife Nicola and our wonderful children, Shaniah, Jaziah, Zakiah and Naphiah. Your beauty, love and support drives me to do all I can to give you all you desire. I thank God for you. I would like to thank my mom and dad for the investment they have made in me over the course of my lifetime.

Big thank you to Neal Brown, Coralie Sawruk, Marcia Jones and Natalie Hemans for your valuable feedback of the first draft of this book. Your feedback helped shape this book and make it what it is. Vinay Patankar, thank you for your foreword. You're a real inspiration to me. I'm glad we've connected. My fellow mastermind members, Peter Billingham, Colin Grey, Mr. Matt Young, Marta Krasnodebska. Your ongoing support has been invaluable. Chris Ducker, I'm humbled to be able to call you my mentor and friend. Your advice has been invaluable. My virtual mentors, Pat Flynn, Jason Van Orden and Jeremy Frandsen, Cliff Ravenscraft, Michael Hyatt, John Lee Dumas and Kate

Erickson, Gary Vaynerchuk, Dan Norris. Thanks to Chris Daniel, you inspired me my brother. Brandy Butler, Audria Richmond, Brad Burton, Leon Streete, Robert Dene Smith, Petra Foster, Herman Stewart, Onyi Anyado, Errol Lawson, Ray Douglas, Juanita Jay Sinclair, Nathan White, Duwayne Fraser.

Thank you also to Mike and Izabela Russell, David Moore, Chris Marr, Michał Szafrański, Kathryn Bryant and Julian Illman, Kelly Long, Rob Lawrence, Sarah Williams, Rob Cubbon, Natalie Silverman, Lee Ball, Emma Victoria and Katrina Burrus. Pastor Paul Williams and his wife Teeky. Phil Gray, Dave Perrin, Joe Jackson, Leroy McConnell, Cheryl McPherson, Barrington Plummer, Morris Cunningham, Sam Henry, Mark Smith.

I'm equally grateful to each and every single person that has supported, encouraged or inspired me throughout the years.

My Sincerest Thanks

Tony

THE ILLUSTRATIONS

I meet Laurens at the New Media Europe conference 2015. When I saw the amazing notes he had produced during the keynotes taking place, I knew I wanted to work with him in one way or another.

Coming from a music industry background, I felt like I had just stumbled across an undiscovered diamond that I knew without a doubt was going to blow up.

Laurens is a sketchnoter, graphic recorder and videoscriber who helps people visualize their ideas so they can communicate those ideas more effectively, help each other to solve problems, and have lots of fun.

He is a true professional who has been a pleasure to work with. I dropped a tight deadline on him, and he delivered the goods, above and beyond my expectations.

Huge thank you, Laurens. You have an amazing talent, and I deeply respect your work. I look forward to working with you on a future project.

Give Laurens a shout on Twitter @laurensbonnema and tell him you saw his work in Standard Procedure.

Visit http://bonnema.ink for more information.

Made in the USA
Charleston, SC
25 April 2016